OHIO SHORT HISTORIES OF AFRICA

This series of Ohio Short Histories of Africa is meant for those who are looking for a brief but lively introduction to a wide range of topics in South African history, politics, and biography, written by some of the leading experts in their fields.

Govan Mbeki

Colin Bundy

OHIO UNIVERSITY PRESS

ATHENS

For Eve

Ohio University Press, Athens, Ohio 45701
www.ohioswallow.com

First published by Jacana Media (Pty) Ltd in 2012
10 Orange Street, Sunnyside
Auckland Park 2092
South Africa
(+27 11) 628-3200
www.jacana.co.za

To obtain permission to quote, reprint, or otherwise reproduce or
distribute material from Ohio University Press publications, please
contact our rights and permissions department at (740) 593-1154
or (740) 593-4536 (fax).

First published in North America in 2013 by Ohio University Press
Printed in the United States of America
Ohio University Press books are printed on acid-free paper ⊚ ™

20 19 18 17 16 15 14 13   5 4 3 2 1

Library of Congress Cataloging-in-Publication Data

Bundy, Colin.
  Govan Mbeki / Colin Bundy.
     p. cm. — (Ohio short histories of Africa)
  "First published by Jacana Media (Pty) Ltd in 2012. First published in
North America in 2013 by Ohio University Press."—T.p. verso.
  Includes bibliographical references and index.
  ISBN 978-0-8214-2046-1 (pb : alk. paper) — ISBN 978-0-8214-4459-7
(electronic)
  1. Mbeki, Govan, 1910–2001. 2. Political activists—South Africa—
Biography. 3. Political prisoners—South Africa—Biography. 4. South
Africa—Politics and government—20th century. I. Title. II. Series:
Ohio short histories of Africa.
  DT1972.M34A3 2013
  968.05—dc23
                              2013001106

Cover design by Joey Hi-Fi

Contents

Govan Mbeki in 1950. (© Robben Island Museum Mayibuye Centre)

Introduction

Intellectual activist –
or activist intellectual?

Govan Mbeki was born on 8 July 1910. The Union of South Africa was barely six weeks old: a new state, delivered by compromise and negotiations at a constitutional conference. Political power was vested firmly in white hands: a limited black franchise operated only in the Cape Province. The Prime Minister was Louis Botha, recently a Boer guerrilla general and now an adroit politician.

Govan died on 30 August 2001. The democratic Republic of South Africa was already seven years old: a fledgling state midwifed by negotiations and concessions at a constitutional conference. Its constitution provided for universal suffrage: electoral power for the black majority was ensured. Its second President was Thabo Mbeki, Govan's eldest son, recently an exiled activist and now an adroit politician.

I like to think that Govan Mbeki might have

twinkled approval of the echoes and comparisons in the paragraphs above. A keen student of history, he frequently drew lessons for the African nationalist struggle from the successes of Afrikaner nationalism. An author and journalist who wrote about politics and economics for over 60 years, he enjoyed finding a telling phrase or instructive detail. And as an acutely political being, he was profoundly aware of just how great were the changes brought to South Africa in the final decade of his long life.

Central to those changes was the part played by the African National Congress (ANC); in turn, the most prominent opponent of the National Party, its negotiating counterpart and its political successor. The ANC may have been founded in 1912, but its key shifts took place from the 1940s onwards. Its history spools out in a dialectical relationship with that of the National Party (NP), elected on an apartheid platform in 1948.

The first NP Prime Ministers, D.F. Malan and Hans Strijdom, largely ignored the ANC, even when it first won a mass base in 1952 with a campaign rejecting the 'unjust laws' of apartheid. H.F. Verwoerd banned the movement in 1960, locked up its leaders and criminalised its every action. B.J. Vorster and P.W. Botha, through the 1970s and 1980s, demonised the exiled body and its army, infiltrated its ranks and bombed its bases. By doing so, they ensured its iconic status in township streets, in classrooms and lecture halls, in hearts and minds. The surging internal resistance spearheaded in the 1980s by the United Democratic Front (UDF) was increasingly explicit in its adherence to an idealised ANC, so that F.W. de Klerk finally decided that it was safer to legalise the movement. He believed that the collapse of Soviet power also weakened the ANC so that it might be outflanked in a negotiated settlement.

And if the ANC's history is central to an account of the liberation struggles waged against white minority rule, Govan Mbeki's politics, career, writings and identity were shaped by a profound commitment to the organisation. Not that he was an apparatchik or uncritical loyalist: far from it. As this biography shows, his long-held and heterodox belief in the political importance of rural people cut little ice in an overwhelmingly urban nationalist movement. Later, his co-authorship of the 'Operation Mayibuye' document was a source of acute controversy. Finally, on Robben Island Govan Mbeki and Nelson Mandela fell out. The two were deeply divided on doctrinal grounds and over strategies, and the gulf was widened by contrasting personalities. Despite these strains, and notwithstanding the extent to which Govan's socialist beliefs imparted a particular spin to his nationalism, he died as he had lived – an ANC standard-bearer. His final request to Dr Mamisa Chabula, his physician and friend, was to be buried in his favourite ANC blanket and cap.

*

I first met Oom Gov in February 1988. Shortly after his release from Robben Island in November 1987, because of his uncompromisingly revolutionary public statements he was subjected to a banning order which restricted his movements and meetings with others. A couple of years earlier, I had written briefly about his political activities in the Transkei during the 1940s; had squirrelled away various pieces of his journalistic output; and was very excited at the prospect of finally meeting, and interviewing, the author of *The Peasants' Revolt*. The meeting was set up by Dullah Omar, then a lawyer in close contact with senior ANC prisoners. I flew from Cape Town to Port Elizabeth where I was met at the airport by a youngish man. He drove me from the airport to a second car; it then whisked me off to a house in Korsten. Govan – I was told – had made his way to the same venue by a similarly circuitous route.

We went to a garage at the end of the driveway where two chairs and a small table had been placed for our interview. Govan motioned me to my chair, but sat himself on the floor, back against the wall, long legs straight out ahead of him. 'I got used to sitting like this on the Island,' he said apologetically, 'but do begin.' And my first memories of the encounter are of the cheap sandals on his feet, which sat oddly with the neatly pressed trousers he wore. That – and his hands: large hands, with long, spatulate fingers, now clasped together as he chased a memory, then alive with gesture, ticking off the points he wanted to emphasise.

When I look now at the transcript of that first interview, I realise that while he was courteous, Govan was also guarded and cautious. It helped that he was familiar with my book on the history of South African peasants – that was why he had agreed to meet me, even though being interviewed for an intended publication transgressed his banning order – but there were topics on which his responses concealed quite as much as they revealed. In subsequent interviews conducted in Port Elizabeth and in Cape Town, the tenor of his responses became warmer, more open. I used to enjoy mentioning something that I had come across in the archives, prompting his surprise – 'now, yes, how did you know that?' – and eliciting that unforgettable, deep laugh. In this book, all direct quotations from Govan are drawn from the transcripts of these interviews; other sources are identified separately.

He was quietly pleased that I was researching his life and wrote to me quite frequently, amplifying remarks he had made, retrieving a forgotten detail, or commenting on drafts of seminar papers. I have to confess that he also used our correspondence to chide me gently, urging me to finish the book. It has taken me a very long time to do so. I hope only that finally it does some form of justice to his life, the life of an activist and of an intellectual, in which activism and intellectualism were not opposites but complementary.

The dining-room table in the Mbeki family home. (Photo by Joanne Bloch)

1

Home comforts and family histories

When Govan Mbeki spoke about his childhood, his face softened and he conveyed a sense of comfort, warmth and stability. The family house – in Nyili village, Mpukane ward, in the Nqamakwe magistracy – was 'a solid house, very well built' and the furniture was handsomely carpentered, 'some of the most beautiful furniture I ever saw'. He spoke with a nostalgic pride about the dining-room table, purpose-built for his father. 'With its extra leaf in, with all its leaves in, it could seat sixteen people – sixteen, all around it. For special occasions, yes.' Even in its more compact form for everyday use, the table would have been ringed by a good number of chairs. Govan had a brother and three sisters – all older than him – and in addition his three half-sisters made extended stays in their father's home. It was a house bustling with women, and one can easily imagine the affection and attention directed towards the *laatlammetjie*. Govan recalled being 'very close' to his mother, and told the film-maker Bridget Thompson that when she attended a wedding, she would tuck a piece of the cake into her *doek* to take home for him: 'And wherever she went, if she got anything nice, she would always bring something home for me.' His sisters also helped raise him, teaching him games and passing on songs they learned at school, and recounting Xhosa fables.

Childhood memories are often rose-tinted. It would be difficult to know, based on Govan's account of his early years, that the family's modest prosperity was being squeezed around the time of his birth; that his ageing father had been dismissed from his post in disgrace; or that, as he grew up, his family would begin a genteel slide: not into outright poverty, but into more straitened circumstances. But before these pressures began to tell, Govan's father, Skelewu Mbeki, was unmistakably a member of a 'progressive' or modernising peasantry that enjoyed its heyday in the Cape Colony and Transkeian Territories in the second half of the 19th century. And like many others at the upper reaches of this peasantry, the Mbeki family was Mfengu; had converted to Christianity; enjoyed modest wealth through a combination of peasant farming and entrepreneurship; and channelled a good portion of its income into a self-consciously modern lifestyle and the best education available for the children.

Skelewu's grandfather, Nonkasa, was an amaZizi herdsman: like many others of that clan, he was swept up in the population movements of the *mfecane*, leaving what is today Bergville district in KwaZulu-Natal. Driven south, Nonkasa was probably among the first few thousand refugees who presented themselves at the Great Place of the Xhosa king, Hintsa, in the 1830s. (When in prison on Robben Island, Govan Mbeki was usually greeted, respectfully, as Zizi – his clan name. But he deflected my questions about the usage, and he consistently sought to underplay references to his ethnicity: 'I would rather you avoid reference to tribal origin,' he wrote to me. I realised only subsequently that Govan – like Oliver Tambo – was highly sensitive to the potential discord that ethnic identities might trigger in the nationalist movement.) Nonkasa entered the Cape Colony in 1836 with two sons, Mfeti and Mbeki, and the latter's seven-year-old son, Skelewu. The family lived briefly near Peddie, then settled close to the Methodist base and school at Healdtown. Here, Skelewu attended school, converted to Christianity, and married another Mfengu convert, with whom he had three daughters.

In 1866 or 1867 Skelewu was among the Mfengu

encouraged by the Cape government to move back across the Kei River and settle in the new British protectorate of 'Fingoland' between the Kei and Mbashe rivers (part of the magistracies of Nqamakwe, Tsomo, Idutywa and Butterworth). Skelewu was accompanied by a number of his amaZizi clanspeople, and they were allocated Mpukane ward (or location, as it was called at the time). Skelewu was recognised at the time as a leader of the ward. 'My father was chief and recognised as such by the people,' Govan Mbeki wrote subsequently. He exercised the authority of a headman for a number of years before his official appointment in July 1890.

It was not only by virtue of office that Skelewu commanded respect in Mpukane. He was also one of the most prosperous men in the ward, and demonstrated this by building a handsome house, built of stone carved by masons at Blythswood mission school. It was (Govan averred) the first stone house owned by an African in the entire district of Nqamakwe. The house stood a few hundred metres from Skelewu's farmland. He owned about 16 morgen of land (or about 30 acres), held under Glen Grey title, but on a plot about four times as large as most Glen Grey land grants. The land was all fenced. In addition to maize and vegetables for household use and for sale, Skelewu raised pigs and poultry. Like other successful peasant farmers, he invested in livestock, and owned goats, sheep, horses and cattle. His cattle herds were too numerous to graze on his own land, and he 'leased' them out in the loan system known as *inqoma*. Selected cattle were fattened on a friend's farm in Komgha district before sale at the King William's Town market. His most profitable enterprise during the 1870s and 1880s was transport-riding. Before the advent of rail and motor lorries, much of the commercial freight in the Cape Colony and Transkei was handled by peasants wealthy enough to own wagons and teams of oxen. Transport-riding was one of the most effective methods of accumulation available to rural households. Skelewu employed drivers who plied his wagons between King William's Town and trading stores across the Transkei.

In 1893 the widowed Skelewu married for a second time. His new wife, Govan's mother, was Johanna Mabula, daughter of a Methodist preacher from Healdtown district. Forty years younger than Skelewu, Johanna bore him five children, three daughters and two sons, Sipho and Govan Archibald Mvunyelwa ('for whom the people sing'). She was an impressive presence in Govan's early life. Fluent in Xhosa, Dutch and English, she was well known in Mpukane. Because of her husband's standing, many local people passed to pay their respects – and Johanna would welcome them with liberality. The visitors did not need to say they were hungry (Govan recalled): 'Whenever you came, the first thing you were offered was food or tea, things like that.'

Headmen like Skelewu were indispensable agents of colonial control, responsible for translating rules and regulations – over land, livestock, travel and taxes – into everyday observance. Their 'loyalty' and 'reliability' were under constant scrutiny; their performance and shortcomings occupy countless pages in the magistrates' records. An instance of this occurred in June 1911. The octogenarian headman Skelewu was fined £10 and dismissed after a hearing conducted by the Nqamakwe magistrate, Gilfillan. The details of the case were not disputed. The headman had infringed the East Coast Fever regulations, restricting cattle movements, having driven five beasts over the Kei in order to sell them to a trader in Stutterheim district. Skelewu knew he was breaking the law. 'I was being pressed for money which I owed. I was tempted by the devil to get the money to pay my debts. I regret my action very much.' The sincerity of the regret cut no ice with the magistrate. He reported that Skelewu 'has been of little use as a Headman owing to old age', and that he had previously been fined for allowing the cutting of trees for firewood with permits.

From the viewpoint of government, the

dismissal was a routine episode in the exercise of local authority. But for Skelewu, his demotion must have been a devastating blow. His entire career had combined loyalty to the colonial state, leadership of his community, and a stern ethical code based on his religious beliefs. Skelewu was a devout Methodist, a teetotaller who said grace before drinking even a glass of water, and a regular contributor to church funds. Govan was not sure of the date his father became a Methodist, 'but the missionaries evidently had great influence on him'. The old man held a prayer meeting every morning at five o'clock, before family members left for school or work; and in the evening the family would gather for an evening prayer, with scripture readings and hymns. One can only imagine the pain caused to Skelewu by the harsh denouement of his career. Govan – who knew nothing of this at the time – remembers spending long hours with his father, whose chair was taken outdoors so that he might sit in the sunshine. 'And I still have a very good picture of him and I loved him' – and he added, tellingly, 'He wasn't a great talker. The stories I heard from my mother's side.'

It is not clear how much formal education Skelewu received, or when, but he wrote correct English in the distinctive 'schooled' script of his generation. But he patently regarded schooling as crucial for his offspring. All eight of his children received secondary education, attending high school at Healdtown. Six (including Govan) qualified as teachers, and Sipho as an agricultural demonstrator. At his death in 1918, Skelewu left savings in separate accounts, specifically for his sons' schooling.

Govan first attended school in 1918. In a family that valued education so highly, he might have commenced a year or two earlier, but he pointed out that geography militated against this. The Methodist school he attended was six miles from the family home, and walking there meant an ascent of the hills that rise from the Tsomo River valley. It was more than a round trip of 12 miles that was involved. The eight-year-old was also taking the first steps in an educational journey that would consume the next 20 years and decisively shape his career as intellectual and activist.

Govan's first educational steps were fortunate in one respect. A government report of 1920 noted that mission schools in Fingoland were superior to most others, a legacy of the days of the first magistrate, Captain Blyth, when 'school attendance was practically enforced by administrative order'. The Wesleyan primary school that Govan attended from the sub-standards through to Standard 6 was built as a church hall and doubled up on weekdays as a one-room school. It was a simple rectangle, with a corrugated iron roof over whitewashed walls. Its only lighting came through its windows.

Years later, Govan recalled it clearly: 'All the classes ranged up the length of the hall, with the highest classes just below the pulpit. The classes sat on either side of the aisle without desks, except for the three more senior forms. Looking back at those days, I often wonder how we managed with each class carrying on its work in the way it saw fit. It was bedlam. One class recited the alphabet, another a multiplication table, a third sang up and down the scale of the modulator, others would be poring over arithmetic problems. The only advantage in the arrangement was that the principal teacher saw his staff at work all the time without having to leave his own class. But little wonder that I was below average in arithmetic!'

Despite the challenging learning environment being described, the sketch is affectionate, not aggrieved. It is a recollection, we may safely conclude, by one who took to reading and writing (if not arithmetic!) with ease. Relevant to Govan's later career as journalist and author, he received a thorough grounding in written and spoken English: 'We started off with English … after passing Standard 6 we talked English according to the grammar book!'

Govan had not completed his first year at primary

school when he fell victim to the influenza epidemic that ravaged South Africa. Nqamakwe was hard-hit, and the Methodist Church noted in 1919 of its Mpukane circuit that 'many have died'. The boy survived his bout, but remembered the severity of his attack: 'I've never been that ill again!' In a single year, the eight-year-old lost his father, survived a fearsome disease and began the daily uphill trudge to the tiny school. This combination might have made school an unsettling experience, associated with illness and death. Not in Govan's case: 70 years later, he spoke warmly of his years in the church-hall school. 'Oh, I enjoyed school. I never played truant! No, I enjoyed it.'

This enjoyment was reinforced by a home life that placed a premium on literacy. Schooling slotted in with the familiar rhythms of the homestead. The daily journey home was downhill; and at its end every afternoon Govan helped herd the livestock into their pens and kraals. Home life and school life overlapped. And at weekends and holidays, Govan and his peers moved with their families' grazing cattle, swam and fished in the Tsomo and Kei rivers, filling their hours with the haphazard intensity of boys at play. Here was an education with a curriculum far older than that on offer in mission schools. Like other African children, Govan acquired (in the words of D.D.T. Jabavu) 'a thorough acquaintance with out-of-door sights of

The house Skelewu built: more than a century later, the Mbeki family home still stands. (Photo by Joanne Bloch)

Mother Nature, games organized by his fellows, the learning of fables and folk traditions … a systematized training in attitudes and behaviour to all elders and superiors … close first-hand familiarity with wild animals, wild trees, wild edible roots: bird trapping … swimming in ponds and streams, riding on goats and calves, and counting the number of cattle and sheep as they return to the fold at the end of each day.'

Govan himself spoke nostalgically of childhood hours outdoors. He recalled with relish walking in the forests of the Tsomo River valley – 'there was fruit, fruit available … growing under natural conditions' – where he heard only birdsong and 'the rustle of the bush and trees', until – thirsty – he knelt at the stream's edge, 'sucking the water from the stream, beautiful, clear, cold'. What was clearly in many ways a delightful childhood world was also a restricted one. Before he went to boarding school, the furthest Govan ever travelled from home was the neighbouring district of Butterworth. He could list his encounters with white people in these years on the fingers of one hand. He had never seen a train until he travelled to Healdtown. Although Nqamakwe lies only 90 kilometres inland, he did not see the sea until he was a young adult. When Govan Mbeki was in his mid-teens, he left home and entered an educational environment more demanding in terms of formal curriculum and less tolerant of the parallel learning. He went to secondary school, as a boarder – not to nearby Blythswood nor to famous Lovedale, both run by Presbyterian missionaries, but to Healdtown, the flagship of the Methodist mission schools.

2

Healdtown and Fort Hare

Pulled from the front, pushed from behind: Healdtown, 1927–1931

In January 1927 Govan Mbeki left his family home for Healdtown, the school founded by the Methodist missionary John Ayliff in 1855. The Healdtown Institution was successively a base for training Wesleyan evangelists, a teachers' training college and an industrial school; but in 1917 a high school was added (attended not only by Govan Mbeki, but also by Nelson Mandela, Robert Sobukwe, Raymond Mhlaba, Seth Mokitimi and other distinguished South Africans). It is set in a valley of the Kat River, below the Mankazana mountains, about seven miles from Fort Beaufort. Like other African boarding schools, it was deliberately located away from urban areas.

Govan travelled from King William's Town to Fort Beaufort by train, its carriages full of students bound for St Matthew's, Lovedale and Healdtown. Older students greeted one another and teased newcomers: for all of them, the experience emphasised a sense of social and generational identity. At Fort Beaufort station, the luggage of those bound for Healdtown was collected (since 1924 by motor lorry instead of ox-wagon!) and the students walked the rest of the way. Phyllis Ntantala was only 12 when she first attended Healdtown – the year Govan left – and recalls arriving 'at eleven o'clock or midnight, tired, dirty and hungry'.

It was a defining feature of the Eastern Cape mission schools that they were boarding schools. To attend Lovedale, Blythswood, Healdtown or their like was not a matter of a daily journey, shuttling between homestead and school-room and learning from each. It was a long-term entry into a rigorously planned and regulated environment, submission to its criteria, and rupture with life outside the school. In a real sense, the journey to boarding school was one to a different society: one with its own structure, hierarchy, laws and subjects. The schools were there to give lessons in the three Rs, certainly, but their intentions were more far-reaching. They wanted to *alter* their pupils, to detach them from their prior identity and equip them with a new one. The Lovedale authorities endorsed the findings of a conference that boarding facilities themselves should help remould their charges: 'The dormitory should be regarded as a training school in which good living habits, high standards in conduct, efficiency in all activities, an appreciation of the value of time, and the ability to cooperate with others are acquired.' The Warden of St Matthew's College (in Keiskammahoek) fretted in 1931: 'When our students come back after a long holiday ... we see a great change in their attitude... We find that when they come back from their holidays ... it takes us some weeks to restore that nice tone which we have been accustomed to ... We teach them manners.'

Healdtown was equally committed to the task of remaking its young subjects. The Rev. J.W. Watkinson was Governor (school principal) when Govan arrived at the school, and he wrote that it had been 'a constant endeavour' to produce a particular kind of boy and girl: 'The tendency of our day to secularise everything has been strenuously resisted, and it has been sought to emphasise the importance of moral character as well as mental equipment, and to inculcate a regard for the amenities and decencies of civilised life' in them. A few years later, Watkinson warned against having young Africans travel for schooling to America: 'They come back with all sorts of subversive and revolutionary ideas.' Healdtown sought instead to ensure that it sent into the world 'the choicest of our young Native people as men, as Christian men, and saturated with Methodism'.

How did the school pursue this project? It put its students in uniforms and established a hierarchy of control rising from the *smongwanas* (new boys) through older pupils and 'captains' (later called prefects) through boarding and teaching staff up to the Governor. It ensured that their every hour was ordered. A Healdtown graduate wryly recalled: 'A rising bell – another for us to line up for breakfast. After breakfast another rang for the commencing of classes – another rang at 11 a.m. to go back to the classes' – and so on until 'Supper first bell was before 6 p.m. … evening study commenced 6.45 …' The students were marshalled into squads for manual work: 'Window cleaners, sweepers … those who offload the wagon …, quarry workers, road workers, cleaning all round the premises, waiters, bread makers' were listed by Joseph Coko, at the school a decade before Govan.

But the full extent of control and concerns is best illustrated by a letter – Foucault meets St Trinian's – written by Watkinson to a Miss Boden the very month Govan arrived at the school: 'Will you kindly enforce the following rules: No girls are to leave the Boarding Department except for school purposes. They must not pass the middle gate in the Avenue until the clock has struck a quarter past eight. No permission is to be given to visit the Location except under very special circumstances … No girls under any circumstances

are to have their meals away from the dining hall …
No variation from the prescribed dietary is allowed for
any girl … Girls may be allowed to go to Stuart's shop
between four and five on Thursday afternoon and at
no other time. No girls are allowed to go to Dick's
shop under any circumstances … All girls speaking
any language except English must be reported to the
Governor. All shouting and screaming must be rigidly
suppressed. No girls are to be allowed through the
gate leading to the bottom camp except on the regular
washing day. The wash house is available for the girls
on Wednesday afternoons and all washing must be
done then.'

Yet Govan Mbeki's own memories of Healdtown
were benign. He relished the academic challenge
and completed his Junior Certificate. His accounts
of those years are couched in warmth and humour.
'Ah,' he ended an anecdote, 'how one has quite – some
nice memories of those days.' Flashes of schoolboy
observation and merriment surface in the interviews.
He mimicked the delivery of the hard-of-hearing Mr
Wellington addressing the students – a heavily stressed
'Wise men learn before experience, fools after'; and
the lilting Welsh cadences of Mr Ball: 'a native child
cannot afford to fail: I am going to pull you from the
front and Mr Caley is going to push you from behind.
You must pass.'

Govan passed. His Junior Certificate subjects were English, Latin, History, Physical Science, Biology and Xhosa. All the tuition was in English, including the Xhosa lessons. He maintained Healdtown's successful record in Junior Certificate passes, performing well enough to win a *Bhunga* scholarship from the Transkeian Territories General Council to proceed to Fort Hare. Yet, even while he buckled down to the demands of the school syllabus, like his contemporaries he was also open to an alternative curriculum. Alongside the pleasures of school life came (as Z.K. Matthews put it) 'the discoveries, slowly accumulating at the same time, of what it meant to be black in a white man's world'. Healdtown – like the other leading mission schools – drew students from all over southern Africa. They pooled information so that the country could be mapped anew. Students learned from each other a topography of racial oppression, shading in local details of injustice, tracing the contours of domination, and poring over possible routes of resistance.

Govan also learned a series of impromptu lessons from the counter-curriculum of experience. In 1925 he attended several concerts organised by a Rev. Mr Mhlongo, of the Independent Methodist Church, in Mpukane. These were fundraising events on behalf of the ANC – the first time he heard of the organisation. A couple of years later, home on holiday from Healdtown, the lanky teenager encountered a more radical politics. His cousin Robert Mbeki was sent to the Transkei by the Industrial and Commercial Workers' Union (ICU) to recruit members and set up branches. Robert opted to speak in English and have Govan, at his elbow, translate his speeches into Xhosa. In 1929 Govan travelled by train to Johannesburg to spend the summer with his half-sister Fanny. It was his first visit to the Rand, his first time outside the rural quietude of the Eastern Cape – and he came face to face with some of the harshest aspects of ghetto life. He saw police raid the yards of City and Suburban for illicit stills and scour the location for pass law offenders. Sixty years after the event, his voice thickened with emotion when he described the menace of the police and the fear of township residents. It 'aroused my anger as nothing else did and determined me to join the struggle to end such a system,' he said. When he left Healdtown to do his Senior Certificate at Fort Hare, he took with him these memories as well as his accomplishments in literature, grammar, Latin and science.

Paying attention to politics: Fort Hare, 1932–1937
For half a century, the South African Native College – its official name, although it was always called

Fort Hare – was the only university for black South Africans. Its propinquity to Lovedale – a couple of miles away, across the Tyhume River – made the small town of Alice the centre of black education in the Eastern Cape. Fort Hare educated many of South Africa's best-known black intellectuals and political leaders in the decades before it was eviscerated as a university by Verwoerd; and the campus was a cradle of assertive African nationalism from the mid-1930s to the late 1950s. It shaped Govan Mbeki profoundly, intellectually and politically. His years there gave him the formal skills that fuelled his output as journalist and author; they also politicised him, deeply and dually.

In the 1930s the campus was a modest cluster of buildings, straddling the road before it crossed the Tyhume into Alice. The college grounds – thick with trees and brush – ran to the banks of the river. This was the setting that Phyllis Ntantala evokes: Fort Hare was 'a beautiful campus, a good and healthy place for young people ... I was young; life was good.' There were about 150 students at Fort Hare, a community small enough for all its members to know one another. As they all lived on campus, it was a close-knit and highly interactive community. Students in the 1930s took their studies seriously, and they also had a range of recreational and social activities. It is unsurprising that those who studied in the 1930s later recalled their Fort Hare days with unmistakable affection.

Govan entered Fort Hare in 1931, his fees covered by a *Bhunga* scholarship worth £28 a year, initially to study for his matriculation. In 1934 he commenced a Bachelor's degree. This required eleven courses: Mbeki did two years of Latin, a year each of English, Xhosa, Ethics and Zoology, and he majored in Psychology and Political Studies (Administration). His choice of subject was significant. 'When we got to Fort Hare students majored in English, most of them in English … Now we became the first group that paid attention to politics, round about 1933, 1934. We ran a campaign against English – against majoring in English – now firstly we attacked the Administration. We said the fellows who taught at Lovedale, Healdtown and of course [D.D.T.] Jabavu at Fort Hare were drawn by the missionaries into their lifestyles so they became sort of black Englishmen … We said fellows must find other subjects to major in, like Political Science.'

Mbeki and McLeod Mabude were the first two students to major in Political Studies. In 1935 Mbeki also completed the requirements for a College Diploma in Education, a post-matriculation teaching certificate. In addition to his studies, Govan served on the Athletic Union, and was secretary of the rugby club. He was very proud of the unbeaten 1935 rugby side, for which he played at lock forward: it was 'the strongest team from Port Elizabeth to Queenstown!' He attended music evenings and learned ballroom dancing. Years later, in solitary confinement in North End prison in Port Elizabeth, he exercised by twirling through the remembered steps with an invisible partner on the cement floor of his tiny cell.

Mbeki credits two people for deepening his political awareness, and for introducing him to Marxism. In the winter of 1933 there took place an encounter he regarded as a decisive political moment in his life. Eddie Roux, a member of the Communist Party of South Africa, and his new bride Win set off on 'a sort of busman's honeymoon'. They had recently begun to bring out a monthly magazine, *Indlela Yenkululeko* (The Road to Freedom), which they dispatched to schools and to Fort Hare. Now, with tents and a donkey, they tramped through the Ciskei – pitching camp by the Tyhume River – and held a series of outdoor meetings. The students (wrote the Rouxs) 'told us of their life in college and of how they were disciplined and treated as schoolboys. We told them of the movement and of *Indlela Yenkululeko*.' Among their audience was a rapt Mbeki, won by the clarity and radicalism of what he heard.

A less likely impetus to left-wing politics came from Max Yergan. Yergan, an African American, worked in

South Africa between 1922 and 1936 as an employee of the YMCA. His biographer has argued that Yergan underwent a 'shift from evangelical Protestantism to revolutionary socialism' in the early 1930s, living 'a double life' (although in later life he became an ultra-conservative and apologist for apartheid). The political conversion may have been later and shallower than in this account. What is clear is that in 1934, on furlough, Yergan visited the Soviet Union and shifted suddenly – and briefly – leftwards. He preached a sermon at the Fort Hare Sunday service, on the text 'I have come that ye may have life, and have it more abundantly' (John 10:10), illustrating this with his impressions of Soviet material progress. Govan grew 'very close' to the black American – who lent Govan books from his holdings of the Little Lenin Library, starting with *State and Revolution*.

Mbeki's interest in socialism – kindled by Roux, fanned by Yergan – became more systematic during his final years at Fort Hare. It took various forms, from student friendships to the distribution of Party literature. For weeks after the Rouxs' al fresco addresses, a small group remained gripped with enthusiasm. Mbeki grew particularly close to a student a year ahead of him, Ernest Mancoba, a gifted artist and witty iconoclast. It was he who took Govan to hear the Rouxs; and afterwards Govan saluted him as 'Comrade Number One'. The pair of them were at the centre of a handful of students who considered themselves socialists: 'it was a small group ... but we were very vociferous.'

Mbeki not only read whatever Marxist material he could lay hands on, but also began distributing it. He bought pamphlets during his summers in Johannesburg, and others were sent to him by Johnny Gomas, a Capetonian and Party member. Such material circulated mainly on campus, but Govan also drove with Yergan into the Ciskeian countryside to spread the word more widely. His visits to Johannesburg brought Govan into contact with Edwin Thabo Mofutsanyana, a leading member of the Communist Party of South Africa (CPSA), whom he greatly admired (and later honoured by naming his oldest Thabo). But he did not join the Party. He explained this to me in terms of his theoretical heterodoxy at the time: his belief that organisational efforts should be primarily in rural areas. 'That was my approach. Let's go and organise in the Transkei, let's go and organise in Zululand, so that when they come to Jo'burg they are already reached – we are able to guide them to take certain actions.' Mofutsanyana (editor of the Party newspaper) was more orthodox, favouring work among urban workers. And (Govan added) 'we used to debate and debate and debate'.

Deciding our future course: New Africanism in the mid-1930s

Govan's interest in socialism and links with individual Party members placed him in a tiny minority at Fort Hare. But this was only one of the political roads he travelled while a student; and in his nationalist excursions he was accompanied by many of his peers. Among his contemporaries were others who left their mark upon South African public life: Nana Honono, A.C. Jordan, Victor Mbobo, Manasseh Moerane, Godfrey Mzamane, Paul Mosaka, Selby Ngcobo, Wycliffe Tsotsi and Benedict Vilakazi. All of them, including Mbeki, were affected by the political culture on campus in the mid-1930s, which reflected a broader phenomenon, a burgeoning sense of African identity, African grievances and African demands. This 'New Africanism' was articulated by members of a black intelligentsia more numerous but less submissive than their parents' generation and structurally distinct from it.

The interwar years saw the growth of an African petty bourgeoisie in South Africa. Proportionately, their tally remained tiny; but in absolute terms they were numerous enough to generate awareness of shared identity and interests. African teachers, clergymen, clerks, nurses and journalists formed professional associations in the 1920s and 1930s.

They experimented with new modes of cultural expression, social practice and political self-reliance – and they did so precisely at a moment, in the mid-1930s, when they felt threatened. Immersed in a world of literacy, learning and modernity, they saw the doors of opportunity previously opened by such immersion being slammed shut. They were alarmed by the loss of the Cape franchise, angered by the growth of segregation embodied in the Hertzog Bills, and frustrated by the impotence of gradualist liberal alternatives and missionary moralising. Their parents had sought through education to win full citizenship in the modern state; but the terms of membership were being rewritten.

The crucial ideological response by African intellectuals to these changes was a re-evaluation and reclamation of the resources and symbols of traditional African culture. The historian Alan Cobley proposes that 'By the 1930s leading members of the black petty bourgeoisie, who, a generation earlier, would have been proud of their attributes and achievements as "black Englishmen", were seeking to affirm their African identities.' This was 'essentially an effort to bring their social origins and their aspirations into harmony with their "Africanness"'. This was not a simple reversion to 'custom' or 'tradition', but attempts to rework African cultural forms and values in 20th-century ways. Thus Albert Luthuli founded a Zulu Language and Cultural Society at Adams College, not from a wish 'to return to the primitive' but 'to preserve what is valuable in our heritage while discarding the inappropriate and outmoded'. Similarly, Z.K. Matthews and Paul Mosaka proposed an African Academy, which would promote 'the serious study of Native problems' as well as produce books on African music and legal systems.

For H.I.E. Dhlomo, 'The new African knows where he belongs and what belongs to him; where he is going and how; what he wants and the methods to obtain it ... [He is] Proud, patriotic, sensitive, alive, and sure of himself and his ideas and ideals ...' Cultural initiatives like these provided material from which a more assertive nationalism could be built in the 1930s and 1940s. The new form of nationalism – announced by the All African Convention (AAC) of December 1935 – was premised on action by Africans for Africans, and not in deferential alliance with white liberals. The new nationalist discourse appropriated the universal terms of liberalism but spoke them with an African accent. It was the language of intellectuals whose politics had been shaped not only in mission schools but also in reaction against them.

Unsurprisingly, similar tendencies were in play at Fort Hare during the 1930s. Govan Mbeki and his contemporaries were less patient and more critical than Jabavu or former ANC Presidents Mahabane and Seme. Their anger peaked during 1935 and 1936. The passage of the Hertzog Bills, the end of the right of African men in the Cape to qualify for the vote, Italy's invasion of Abyssinia and excitement about the All African Convention were the issues that seized the young men and women at Fort Hare. In an obituary for one of his classmates, Benedict Futshane, Govan wrote that 1936 was 'a year that decided the future course of most of us then at Fort Hare'. Like many of his classmates, Govan became a member of the ANC in that year. They were (he said) 'absolutely moved' as these events 'whipped up so much feeling'. The intimate geography of Fort Hare meant that students could debate and argue over meals, in the dormitories, between classes, and in hastily convened meetings. 'And those of us who were already drawn into political life' (commented Govan), 'well, during holidays we were taking part in meetings – especially in Jo'burg.'

The New Africanism found various expressions on campus. Students protested successfully against a segregated entrance at the Alice post office, and, with staff members, challenged segregated seating at a Lovedale athletics meeting. A.C. Jordan wrote a poem in Xhosa denouncing the Italian invasion of Abyssinia. Paul Mosaka led a protest against the employment of white women as domestic workers when there were so many unemployed African women in Alice. And alongside these overtly political forays, Mbeki and his peers set out to reclaim and rework elements of African culture. They travelled to Ntab'ozuko near King William's Town, to hear the famous Xhosa poet S.E.K. Mqhayi recite *izibongo*. I asked Phyllis Ntantala to explain the enthusiasm of her Fort Hare circle for Xhosa epic poetry: she replied that they were engaged in a broader project of cultural reclamation. They 'were beginning to question some of the myths on which they had been fed, and beginning to see the old people in the villages to find out what happened this year and that'. Although Govan Mbeki loved English and Latin poetry, he venerated Mqhayi. He started a novel while a student, and completed a play which he submitted to the Lovedale Press. Both were written in Xhosa. His favourite Latin poet was Catullus: 'I found it so interesting and started very quietly translating into Xhosa.'

Latin poetry and the Little Lenin Library. Wordsworth on Westminster Bridge and Mqhayi on his hill-top. Secretary of the rugby club and in the same year a new member of the ANC. These were just some of the elements that constituted Govan's experience of Fort Hare. He was representative of a new strain in Fort Hare's student politics. He and others sought to reconcile their education and their aspirations with their frustration and their Africanism. Their fluency in English – says Cobley – carried implicit social, cultural and political attitudes, 'but the framework of meaning was provided by their experience as an emerging class in racist South Africa'. Command of the colonial language (which was also the language of colonial command) was one element in their repertoire. Calling upon an African national identity (which meant identifying with the call of nationalism) was another, indispensable component.

Skelewu Mbeki, as we have seen, was determined that his younger son should be educated; and Govan was gripped by education and its pleasures. But his own ties to Mpukane seem to have worn thin during his years at Healdtown and Fort Hare. He spent more time on the Rand than in the Transkei. He and his brother Sipho had fallen out, over the expense of Govan's education. In 1935 his mother died. Yet when he can have least expected it, village matters impinged on his life. A new headman was to be appointed in Mpukane ward. While a sizeable faction of amaZizi villagers favoured having another Mbeki as headman, they knew that the Nqamakwe magistrate did not favour Sipho Mbeki. And so they nominated Govan for the post. The magistrate was dubious. He considered Govan too young and believed that 'it is very doubtful whether he would take up the appointment', but approached Govan, by then teaching in Natal. Govan made a trip home; spoke to some of the elders; and tried unsuccessfully to persuade the magistrate to appoint a regent until Sipho's son was old enough to take the reins. He had no desire to take the post himself. He had a degree (he pointed out) and was earning more than the pittance paid to a headman.

The episode was not an important one in Govan's life. He never mentioned it; and laughed, surprised, when I raised it in an interview: 'Yes, that was – how did you get that?' Unimportant, perhaps; yet as one contemplates the pattern of his life, it is a telling moment. It coincided with his move from formal education to employment; it demarcates the difference between his father's horizons and his own; and it reinforces the sense of how the young graduate had been shaped by school and university. The magistrate was right to suppose that Govan was unlikely to accept the post if it were offered to him. He had been schooled beyond it: emotionally, intellectually and politically.

3

Permanent persuader

Mbeki in the Transkei, 1940–1952

In 1937, having graduated from Fort Hare, Govan Mbeki applied for a teaching post at the Taylor Street Secondary School in Durban. The school had been founded in 1921 to educate the children of the 'Married Quarters', housing set aside just north of the city centre for the families of African Christian converts. It was in the staff-room here that Govan met a fellow teacher, 22-year-old Epainette Moerane. She was born to a leading family in the Sotho-speaking community of Mount Fletcher district in the Transkei. Her parents were Christians, modernisers, active in the Catholic Church, successful peasant farmers, and – it hardly needs saying – strongly committed to securing the best available schooling for their children. Piny, as her friends and family called her, had moved from the nearby boarding school at Mariazell, to Lovedale and then to Adams College near Durban, where she completed her teacher training.

She recalls her first impressions of Govan: unostentatious, reserved, rather lonely – 'particular about how he dresses, particular about how he speaks'. It is a pity that Govan did not provide a matching memory, and in its absence one can only surmise what he made of his new colleague. Piny was tiny but formidable: 'a thoroughly modern, thoroughly independent woman', outside teaching hours 'fully occupied with activist work', as Mark Gevisser notes. Her political awareness, she said, began in 1935–6, with the Hertzog Bills. And it was indeed politics that drew the two of them together. They did not begin courting at first – she stressed – but 'it just came naturally because we were both interested in bettering things'. She recalled their conversations in Durban: 'We talked a lot of politics. We talked a *lot* of politics.' Govan concurred. Their friendship and subsequent marriage were 'largely influenced by the fact that we thought alike'.

Piny became a member of the Communist Party in Durban, recruited in 1938 by Bettie du Toit, who grew close to Govan too. Other Party members with whom the two young teachers spent time were George and Vera Poonen. Govan moved from the Taylor Street School in 1938 to teach Latin at Adams College, the premier African school in Natal. Edgar Brookes (who had moved from being a proponent of segregation to its liberal critic) was Principal, assisted by Donald Mtimkulu – and although their politics diverged, Govan recalled both men warmly. 'I was very happy with them. They understood me.' Although teachers at Adams were normally required to lead prayers, Brookes and Mtimkulu accepted Govan's break with the church and exempted him from this duty. He taught in the mornings: 'But in the afternoon I was back in Durban, active in my politics.'

Towards the end of the year, Govan received a telegram inviting him to take a teaching post at Clarkebury, a mission school in Engcobo district in the Transkei. He jumped at the chance – and the decision prompts a question. Why would this highly educated and politicised young man leave Durban for a rural backwater? In later life, Govan always answered this question by directing those who asked it to a passage in his booklet called *Transkei in the Making*. The Transkei had produced more Fort Hare graduates than any other region, 'but where are they? What is the purpose of educating these young fellows if, after the completion of their particular studies, they are not to come to the territories and apply the knowledge which they have acquired at so much public cost to the problems which ever become more and more complicated?'

Mbeki answered this question for himself by

moving back to the Transkei: initially as a teacher at Clarkebury (but dismissed after 18 months for his political work and robust secularism) and subsequently as storekeeper, journalist, political organiser and activist. He was also a husband and a father. He and Epainette were married in January 1940 and four children were born between 1941 and 1948: Linda, Thabo, Moeletsi and Jama. Mark Gevisser has written with insight and sympathy about the Mbekis' family life during the 1940s: a marriage increasingly strained; a household teetering on the edge of solvency; Epainette's activism and idealism submerged by the slog of everyday existence ('I had to take care of everything'); Govan frequently absent and, even when he was at home, holed away with his books and his writing, too busy to read to his children – 'I pushed them to their mother'.

This chapter does not seek to enlarge on the domestic stresses detailed by Gevisser. Instead, it traces the development of Mbeki's political ideas, using his writings at the time, and then assesses his political activities during the years he spent in Idutywa.

Study with a definite purpose: Mbeki as commentator and thinker, 1938–1948

Govan's earliest publication was *Transkei in the Making*, written in 1938, primarily as a response to a

publication by Howard Pim, *A Transkei Enquiry, 1933.*
Although published as a booklet in 1939, it appeared
originally in eight parts in *New Outlook*, a short-
lived monthly edited by Edgar Brookes. It still makes
fascinating reading, not only as a commentary on
the social and economic conditions of the Transkei,
but also as a series of signposts to the intellectual and
political route Mbeki was travelling.

Pim was a Quaker and prominent liberal. One
can only imagine how the young Mbeki was irked
by Pim's unselfconscious paternalism. 'The Bunga
appeals strongly to the dramatic sense of the Bantu,'
he opined; and concluded that 'this attractive race,
for which we have made ourselves responsible' was
capable of development; they 'are showing a real
capacity for advance, even though it is slow'. Mbeki
explicitly rejected Pim's explanation that Africans
were backward because of cultural conservatism,
arguing that 'statements such as "they do not like to
change" go a long way towards establishing a national
economic attitude towards the black man's standard of
living'. He sought to provide an alternative explanation
for the lack of economic development in the Transkei.

The booklet opened up issues to which Mbeki
would return again and again: economic difficulties
confronting African peasants, the political economy of
the Reserves, a critique of chiefs and headmen ('in the

Bunga's cosy chairs at Mtata … they represent nobody but themselves'), and the importance of education. *Transkei in the Making* is the work of a young man. Although the prose is controlled and formal, its flow is interrupted every so often by an eddy of radicalism. For instance, the famous meeting in 1848 between the Cape Governor Sir Harry Smith and the Xhosa chiefs is summarised thus: 'There unarmed indigenous social structure was threatened to its knees by British capitalistic ravenousness backed up by cannon.' Laws to drive labour to the cities and mines 'have hastened the coming of general poverty – inescapable poverty; poverty which is not confined to any one class but covers us all, and is passed on from generation to generation'. The final sentences run: 'Africans will not mistake half measures for full ones. In the pursuit of the object for which this essay has been written fanaticism alone is good enough.' There are echoes of the Marxism which had influenced Mbeki at Fort Hare. The 'rigours and vices' of a capitalist society should not be deliberately imported into the Transkei so as to create 'that most iniquitous system which will enable a chosen few to be possessors of all the means of production'. There is mention of 'the potential powers which lie latent in the African labouring masses', but these points were not developed.

When the series ran in *New Outlook*, Mbeki was

approached by P.K. Bonga and P.C. Katamzi, who ran a small printing press in Verulam, Natal. They offered to publish the articles as a booklet, and had a further proposal: 'Then we want to start a paper. We will give you all the freedom to express your ideas – all that we are interested in is that the paper should be there, so that it advertises our services.' The paper was launched as *The Territorial Magazine* and by June 1938 Mbeki was listed as editor. In this capacity (he told Dr Xuma, ANC Treasurer, in 1940) he was 'writing the leaders, the sub-leaders, and other articles'. In May 1940 the paper was renamed *Inkundla ya Bantu* (Bantu Forum). It remained, until its demise in 1952, the only significant newspaper owned and run by Africans. It circulated mainly in Natal and the Transkei and on the Witwatersrand. In the early 1940s Cuthbert Motsemme became the major partner in the concern, and he approached a fellow ANC Youth Leaguer, Jordan Ngubane, to become the new editor. Ngubane was determined to use the paper to raise the profile of the Youth League; he also stamped his antipathy to the Communist Party on the paper. But from 1938 until August 1943, *Inkundla* was a conduit for Govan Mbeki's views; an invaluable source for understanding his politics; and the arena where he first tested key elements of his later and better-known writings.

Mbeki's nationalism

In interviews after his release from Robben Island, Govan distanced himself from the ANC Youth Leaguers and their fervent Africanism: 'No, I couldn't be part of the Youth League. My thinking was different from theirs. Mine was a Marxist approach, and theirs was purely nationalistic.' But in *Inkundla* he not only displayed a conscious and robust nationalism, but at times did so in unambiguously Africanist tones. He was entirely representative of his times. A striking ideological innovation of the later 1930s and early 1940s was a generalised tendency among the educated elite of an Africanist vocabulary and self-definition. This was true, we have seen, for Govan's contemporaries at Fort Hare. They, and other black middle-class intellectuals, shared a profoundly unsettling experience. In greater numbers than their parents, they had been fully exposed to the prevailing 'high culture', an exposure that carried the promise of integration and acceptance; but that promise had been abruptly curtailed. And, of course, the New Africanism found organisational expression in the formation of the Youth League.

It was also unmistakably present in Govan's writings at the time. He dedicated *Transkei in the Making* 'To the Youth of my Race'. As editor of *Inkundla*, he stressed its African ownership and its commitment to African interests: 'Our duty has always been, ever is, and shall always be to the African people first.' No issues, he wrote, can 'make us, for a moment, forget our main purpose – struggle for national liberation'. One of his first editorials was entitled 'The Task Ahead of Us'. It began by looking back, through a nationalist lens. It was 100 years since the defeat of Dingaan in 1838, and (he wrote) 'I would like to take this opportunity of paying tribute to those men (I refer to Moshesh, Tshaka, Hintsa and their no less reputable followers) who out of that Godly nature in them, love for freedom, freedom according to the ways they understood and defined it, seized the most primitive weapons to defend that natural right … These remain the greatest figures in our living memory.'

In 1941 Mbeki launched an ambitious and classically nationalist project. *Inkundla*, he wrote, would create a 'Gallery of African Heroes', short biographies of men and women who advanced the African cause; readers were urged to submit contributions; a successful series would 'certainly be the African People's History in the Making'. The gallery's first hero was Hintsa, the Xhosa king, and the piece was written by Mbeki himself. He used existing histories, like Macmillan's *Bantu, Boer and Briton*, but drew too on Mqhayi's epic verse. Heroic, moving, didactic: the biography

Govan Mbeki on the Xhosa king Hintsa

The making of big historical events is usually not confined to one locality. Hintsa ... a contemporary of Napoleon, belonged to the big Trio of African kings – Moshesh, Tshaka and Hintsa ... Hintsa lived and ruled at a time when Britain was feverishly forging her empire with iron and fire ... In the Cape the British governors were entering into short lived treaties with the Xhosa Chiefs, but the desire to build an empire was so overwhelming that such treaties were blown to the winds with the flimsiest of excuses. Times were generally unhappy. Ntsikana, the Great Prophet, had prophesied such times, and in truth they came. The poet-laureate, *Imbongi yeSizwe*, had declared like Bismarck: 'The world is sick' (*Izwe liyazuza*) ...

[Hintsa's rule rested on] the natural democratic principles which are to be found among the less developed societies of mankind. [A lover of peace, Hintsa] was charged by the gods with the duty of leading his people in military operations against those who violated the integrity of his sphere of existence ... It was

> not until the impetuous Sir Harry Smith that
> the end of this great man was at once to come.
> [Smith held Hintsa hostage and sought to use
> him to persuade other chiefs to surrender.] The
> choice was now between betraying his people
> and facing death ... he made a dash for freedom
> and he was shot dead and his body mutilated.
>
> Such is the end of those who love freedom,
> for freedom is God's greatest gift to mankind.
> He was born in a land of freedom, he lived and
> breathed the free air in a free land. When his
> freedom and that of his people was threatened
> there was nothing else left for him but to risk
> the British bullets ... Hintsa died free that his
> people might have freedom and have it more
> abundantly.

exemplifies nationalist discourse. It asserts Hintsa's modernity, his fall at the hands of a greedy empire, and celebrates him as a heroic martyr to liberty.

This kind of nationalist history does not prescribe a particular kind of organised nationalist politics. So how did Mbeki locate himself vis-à-vis the ANC and the All African Convention (AAC) in these years? An ANC member since 1935, he shared the Youth Leaguers' impatience with the tactics and vision of the older leadership. Africans must choose 'between two ways': that of the last hundred years or a fresh start. The ANC and AAC should 'stop and examine their machinery thoroughly', retaining anything useful but discarding formal, empty elements. A favoured dismissive epithet was 'Victorian'; and he blamed an outmoded adherence to Cape liberalism for inappropriate levels of deference and accommodation. Perhaps the closest that Mbeki moved to a Youth League position was in January 1942. The 'old men of Victorian liberalism' could not deal with 'forces born of modern power'. He welcomed 'rumours of African youth organisations': it was 'necessary, nay, very urgent' that younger people should seize control of the 'present moribund African National organisations' and turn them into working concerns rather than honour-conferring affairs.

Mbeki's Marxism

Yet, despite the convergence between Mbeki's nationalism and that of men like the Youth Leaguers Anton Lembede, A.P. Mda and Jordan Ngubane, the picture is more complex if one considers a second major element in Mbeki's writings in this period: his Marxism. In addition to the young nationalist (and sometimes in the same article) is the scholar with a degree in Economics who believed that 'the fundamental problem of the African people is economic'. Govan registered in 1937 for an Economics degree with Unisa, awarded in 1941; he did so because he found Bukharin's writings interesting but difficult! Mbeki's Marxism involved no quotations from Bukharin, Lenin, Marx or other authorities. There is an occasional formulaic proposition: 'History teaches that in his development, man has to pass through the hunting, pastoral, agricultural and industrial stages respectively.' But for the most part, Mbeki sought to understand economic processes and structures; to apply concepts of class formation and class conflict to South African life; and to follow an epistemology that accorded some form of primacy to economic factors in human life. In addition to his writings for *Inkundla*, Mbeki also wrote in the 1940s for the left-wing papers *Inkululeko*, edited by his old friend E.T. Mofutsanyana, and the *Guardian* (he was a Contributing Editor and a member of the Editorial Board, respectively, for these publications).

Two lines of argument run through a number of the pieces Mbeki wrote in these years: analysis of the Reserve economies and advocacy of trade union organisation. Two articles on overstocking were written in 1938, relating cattle numbers directly to the impoverishment and proletarianisation of Reserve peasants. Land in the Transkei held in terms of the 1936 legislation 'is more for dumping purposes than for economic relief – it is labour reserves'. The fundamental difficulty, he warned, 'is the anomaly of White capital and Coloured labour in South Africa ... We repeat that so long as the Native Reserves are regarded as a reservoir of cheap labour, so long will overstocking continue.' Mbeki linked the drive for the culling of cattle to the emergence of a collaborating 'traditional' elite as a new class. The culling proclamation allowed chiefs, headmen and councillors to accumulate cattle. This was 'a vicious conversion of the good old communal ownership of property ... into a handy weapon for the Government to divide and rule'.

Mbeki attempted more generally to analyse African society in terms of its class composition. He identified four major 'economic groups': urban workers, farm workers, Reserve-based peasants, and a 'floating population' of migrant workers. These were men without land, who must supplement peasant income with wages. Graphically, he summed up the migrant's existence 'like a frog that partly spends its life on land and partly in water' – and in more formal Marxist terminology as 'a large reserve labour army', whose existence would depress African wages generally. The most forceful and explicitly Marxist commentary on the Reserves was penned by Mbeki in 1945 in a four-part series in the *Guardian* in response to the announcement of a scheme for the 'rehabilitation' of the Reserves. He pointed out that the proposed 'rural villages' would 'create a hitherto unknown social group', a full-blown rural proletariat, in the Reserves: 'it means the branding and sifting of migratory labour and dumping it in one spot.' The villages would serve the same function as a garage for a car: 'to repair and overhaul the worker so that he will be a fit tool in the service of those who must exploit his power to work.'

Another recurrent theme was the necessity for trade union organisation. An *Inkundla* editorial of October 1940 made the case in straightforward and conventional terms. Industrial development had 'split society into two camps whose interests are irreconcilable'. Employer and employee stood in two different camps; the former's sole concern the 'accumulation of profits with the least possible expenditure'; the latter 'the earning of a wage which will enable him at least to guarantee continued existence'. The first weapon of defence available to workers was organisation into trade unions. Primarily concerned with trade unions for African workers, Mbeki sometimes argued the case in terms of the working class as a whole. 'To protect their own interests, the WORKERS, irrespective of race and colour must form TRADE UNIONS.' He spelled out the difficulties confronting those who would organise African workers, but urged bodies like the ANC and AAC to do all in their power to encourage trade unions. Low wages paid to unorganised industrial workers depressed wages and salaries in other sectors: 'Trade unions fight your battles, support them.'

A separate strand in Mbeki's economic thinking was the potential of co-operative ventures. In *Transkei in the Making* there is a tentative advocacy of co-operative farming, suggesting groups of peasants might pool resources to buy a tractor. The Mbekis' shop at Mbewuleni was initially opened as a co-operative (though the other partners fell away). In 1944 his booklet *Let's Do It Together* appeared in the Sixpenny Library series written in 'basic English' and edited by Eddie Roux. The idea of co-operation was not new to Africans, he pointed out: the practice of *iLima* in rural areas saw reciprocal help in ploughing and building homesteads; and in cities the *stokvel* provided purchasing power to individuals through collective savings. He made the case for co-operative credit societies ('Poor people can own a bank'!), for collective purchasing by peasant farmers and co-operative marketing of their produce. Addressing the Cape African Teachers' Association, Mbeki linked co-operative ventures to a broader social and political purpose: by working together economically, people could not only improve their material condition but also 'move on to their goal, self-emancipation'.

Unsurprisingly, Mbeki also wrote frequently about education. There is a striking warning – 15 years before Verwoerd's Bantu Education Act – that education could be used to stifle and block African advance: 'the interests of those who form the ruling class' decisively shaped the schooling of the black races. 'In educating the African care is being taken that he is given only such education as will fit him for a position which is forever subservient.' Time and again, Mbeki stressed the purpose of education as well as its content. Knowledge for its own sake was a limited good. Study was not an end in itself: 'study must be carried on with a definite purpose to work out a better future for ourselves and our children.'

A striking editorial made the case for the relevance of history and the social function of knowledge. 'A better understanding of our past historical development is essential, a clearer interpretation of the historical facts that have led to the present position of the Africans is urgent. A clear grasp of the problems which confront us today is impossible without a clear understanding and interpretation of the facts that made our forefathers put away their shields and spears, our fathers carry kits on their backs to seek hard fortunes on the diamond and gold mines …

'Where do we, the present generation stand? We stand on the shattered ruins of a once African social structure. We are living in chaotic times where it becomes, daily, exceedingly difficult to grasp the problem in its wholeness. We are inclined to see it in dissociated parts, and that makes it impossible for us to find a solution ... If we are to seek a solution to a problem we must be fully acquainted with its entire nature, we must pull apart the component parts and analyse them carefully and find their relation one to the other. To say "we must organise" is profitless, if we do not know what to organise for.'

This raises the relationship between consciousness and agency or, as older Marxist texts put it, the unity of theory and practice. Let us turn, then, from this outline of Govan Mbeki's writings to an account of his activities. What was he organising for?

Throwing everything into the fire:
Mbeki as organiser, 1940–1948

While he was still a student at Fort Hare, Mbeki met Dr Xuma, then Treasurer of the ANC, several times during his visits to Johannesburg. In 1937 the tall young graduate visited the diminutive doctor and asked for employment as an ANC organiser. He had worked out that he could live on £8 a month and offered his services at this modest rate. Xuma responded avuncularly: 'Govan, my dear man – first make money before you go into politics!'

Mbeki failed signally to follow this advice. By 1940 his teaching career included two dismissals on political grounds; and the co-operative store at Mbewuleni never resembled the financial launch-pad advocated by Xuma. Yet Mbeki went into politics almost from the outset. During 1940, his first year in Idutywa, his public activities were focused on promoting co-operative credit societies. But in October 1941 he was elected Secretary of the Transkei African Voters' Association (TAVA), a body with structures in every district, and chaired by Charles Sakwe. Mbeki had worked with Sakwe in the co-operative credit movement, and respected him; the older man quickly recognised the abilities of his young colleague.

Mbeki was well aware that the ANC had only a tenuous presence in the Transkei: as he put it in a letter to Xuma, 'The Transkei is, to be frank, politically in mid-night slumber.' Throughout the 1940s, his efforts were aimed at breaking that slumber, prodding the Transkei awake. But he had clear views on how most effectively to link his organisational efforts in the Transkei with national campaigns mounted by a body like the ANC. Firstly, he was convinced of the power of the printed word and the value of an agitational press. He saw his *Inkundla* leaders and articles as part of his

62

political project. He tried several times, unsuccessfully, to persuade Xuma that the ANC should take over *Inkundla* as its own publication, under its control. He greeted Xuma's election as President-General in 1940 with a welcoming front-page lead (subtitled 'Dr Xuma puts on boots'!) – and slipped in some editorial advice. Xuma's foremost duty was to 'draw the professional classes into better understanding of the working classes and their conditions'; and (added Mbeki) 'Dr Xuma will require a newspaper that will further his policy – that is absolutely essential.'

Secondly, he chose to work within existing local organisations rather than trying to create new Congress branches. TAVA was the initial base from which he built a more substantial organised presence in the region's politics. TAVA was a key body representing the Transkei's elite, and, with Mbeki as its new Secretary, it rapidly adopted a more radical stance. At its annual meeting in December 1942, TAVA passed a vote of no confidence in the *Bhunga* (Transkeian General Council) representatives and called for sweeping changes to Hertzog's 1936 segregatory legislation. The franchise for Africans should apply equally to men and women, and Africans in other provinces should have the same rights as those in the Cape. It also convened a conference 'of all organised bodies in the Transkei' to decide on priorities and to 'present their demands' to government. And six weeks later, over a hundred delegates launched the Transkeian Organised Bodies (TOB). 'Cutting across tradition' (noted *Inkundla*) women delegates were on an equal footing with men. Delegates came from farmers' organisations, co-operative societies, Vigilance Associations, welfare societies, a trade union, a Social Studies club and two women's organisations. The TOB significantly ratcheted up the level of mobilisation in the Transkei, linking a range of disparate interests into a single, co-ordinated pressure bloc.

Thirdly, the decisive next step from strengthening local structures was to link them to policies and campaigns at the national level, led by the ANC. By October 1943, Govan told an interviewer that 'the pulse of the Transkei is quickening encouragingly' and that he sought to organise the region's voters 'into a solid block of "loyal and politically conscious members"'. A year later he explained that TAVA had reached a new stage in its history. It could no longer rely on spasmodic 'finely worded petitions' but should prepare 'to fight decisive battles in these territories and to prepare for cooperation on a national scale'. Local politics fed into broader forms: 'people must be interested in more immediate issues and thus gradually link them up with the national struggle'. Start with local issues; build a corps of 'loyal and politically conscious members'; and then 'gradually link them up with the national struggle' – this was the essence of Mbeki's strategy, then and subsequently.

Between 1943 and 1948, Mbeki was almost ceaselessly active in politics based on this approach. In 1943 the TOB entered a national campaign against the pass laws. Inaugurated by the Communist Party, the project was enthusiastically greeted in urban areas and assisted by Xuma's agreement to chair the Anti-Pass Council. Mbeki wrote articles and made speeches denouncing the pass laws; he attended an anti-pass conference in East London and was elected there to represent the Eastern Cape on the national Anti-Pass Council. The TAVA and TOB both declared solidarity with the campaign, at meetings where a newly composed Anti-Pass Hymn was sung. As Mbeki set about raising funds in the Transkei for the national effort, he called for new levels of commitment: 'We have to bend our all to the fulfilment of our one goal – the repeal of the pass laws – for which we shall require faith, hope, and above all, courage.' But national leadership of the campaign proved irresolute, and the movement spluttered to an anti-climactic end. In December 1946 the ANC annual conference rebuked Xuma by voting that it was 'deeply dissatisfied' with the conduct of the campaign.

The collapse of the campaign in the cities left

its supporters in the countryside deflated. Four and a half decades later, Govan Mbeki told me of the excitement that the campaign had generated in the Transkei, and then continued wryly: 'Now what happened? The National Executive of the ANC called off the campaign through the *Guardian*. It had not informed us at the lower levels. It makes a statement in the *Guardian* that the campaign has been called off. In the meantime, we are still continuing and telling the people there is this campaign. This is one of the issues on which I took strong exception to Dr Xuma at the time.'

In 1947 Mbeki and his Transkei colleagues were left even more awkwardly stranded by the ANC leadership. In December 1946 the ANC decided to boycott all parliamentary and Natives Representative Council elections – and in 1947 applied this policy to a parliamentary by-election in the Transkei. Here was a national campaign focused on Transkeian politics. Govan flung himself and his organisations into it unreservedly: 'we were throwing everything into the fire', he reported to Xuma; the Transkei was 'up and doing'. But Xuma now backtracked on the policy, proposing a symbolic 'write-in' vote for African candidates instead. Govan demurred, pointing out the impracticality of the plan. He was worried that the ANC seemed to be dragging its feet. 'What plans are you developing to clamp down on Advisory Boards, Councils and individual chiefs?' He spelled out his anxieties: 'Writing a letter like this I feel I must be frank. Our fears here are that we may work up the people only to find that the rest of the country does not attach much significance to its resolutions. Country folk have a way of being honest. We have already lost face in the Anti Pass Campaign which was just dropped when we were working up the people ... That should not happen again in this affair unless we must risk a setback for a decade or more.'

Even while the TOB and TAVA rededicated themselves to the boycott strategy, the ANC leadership prepared to ditch it, overriding the objections of the Youth Leaguers at the 1947 annual conference. The volte-face impacted on the Transkei, where so much energy had been spent on the boycott. A contest took place for control of the TOB – and it was one which Govan Mbeki was to lose. In 1948 a new executive was elected; Mbeki was replaced as Secretary; and by the year's end the TOB had affiliated to the AAC, under the fiery leadership of I.B. Tabata, founder and President of the Non-European Unity Movement. Boycott was the AAC's central tactic: it could claim a consistency that the ANC had forfeited. Mbeki was also criticised by Tabata for having spent a term as a *Bhunga* member: an ill-judged and futile effort to influence that body from within.

Govan had been at Fort Hare with several of the AAC Transkei activists: Wycliffe Tsotsi, Nana Honono, Victor Hermanus and C.M. Kobus. In the early 1940s, he shared political enthusiasms with this group and socialised with them despite their respective affiliations. By his own account, when Govan first became active in TAVA he 'worked with people ... who were largely under the influence of the ... Unity Movement'. As the decade progressed, tensions between the AAC and ANC mounted, and were replicated in the Transkei. Govan found himself increasingly at odds with Tabata and with the local AAC leaders, and by 1948 recognised that he had been outflanked.

The permanent persuader

It was a political defeat, but within the wider context of his political career the years spent in the Transkei were crucial ones. They saw sustained intellectual and political activism, and considerable organisational success with scant resources. Govan's role in radicalising Transkeian politics was palpable. The TOB enlarged the scale of rural opposition to the state; and the popular militancy shown in the anti-pass and boycott campaigns deserved greater support from the ANC leadership than it received. These years were Govan's political apprenticeship. His subsequent reputation (as 'an ANC kingpin in the Eastern Cape ... organiser, propagandist, technician, policy-maker, man of action and intellectual') was well earned; but his role in Port Elizabeth a few years later cannot be understood without prior appreciation of his efforts to rouse the Transkei and his zest at living 'when history is being made all around us'.

This chapter has not attempted to provide a full history of political activism in the Transkei in the 1940s. It has concentrated on Mbeki's role. His politics were institutional. He used the press; worked in identifiable organisations; and mounted systematic campaigns linked to national programmes. Popular radicalism was different: less structured, less explicit, often covert, and primarily local. Yet each influenced the other. Impulses flowed up and down. Mbeki's exertions took place in the context of a rolling, rumbling swell of rural resentment during the 1940s and 1950s. This sometimes spilled into open insurgency; more typical were less dramatic, more dispersed forms of resistance. Reserve dwellers in South Africa lacked the social power to mount frontal attacks on the sources of their subordination; their forms of protest lay largely beyond the gaze of the state. Recent scholarly work (by Crais, Gibbs, Ntsebeza, Redding and others) has revealed a good deal about the undercurrents of popular resistance in the Transkei in the 1940s, 1950s and early 1960s. We know something of how widespread, protracted and desperate were localised struggles by Transkeians to protect their land and livelihoods, to evade controls over how they should plough and fence their land or dip and cull their cattle, and to reject controls by chiefs and headmen.

Mbeki's political register was institutional, formal and overt. Yet it was also influenced by popular political cadences – informal, hidden, local, coded and cautious. One way in which Govan was in contact with ideas from below was the trading store. His customers were predominantly illiterate, red-blanketed *amaqaba* people. Mbeki not only sold items to them, but mixed with them: Gevisser mentions him 'singing and practising traditional dances with his neighbours outside the shop'. In June 1941, a visitor to Mbewuleni store described it thus: 'The man behind the counter has much work, wrapping, weighing, cutting, measuring, selling, persuading and last but not least talking to the people … he must speak to people about their lowly location affairs in a friendly spirit [and] encourage them in their undertakings.'

Epainette Mbeki, when I interviewed her, conveyed something very similar. I asked whether her husband became caught up with local politics and she replied:

'Some people who come here, they bring their small problems ... Sometimes somebody wants to start a business, or somebody wants to go to these industrial areas and seek for work, doesn't know what steps to take. You know, such problems ... Somebody gets injured in Johannesburg and they don't know where to go for compensation – such like. And somebody's cattle will get ill. They don't know what to do, what medicine to use. All sorts of problems.'

This snapshot of Mbeki – 'measuring, selling, persuading and ... speaking to the people' – calls to mind Gramsci's definition of an organic intellectual, one whose mode consisted not in mere eloquence 'but in active participation in practical life, as constructor, organiser, "permanent persuader"...' Speaking to the people also meant listening to the people. In 1947 *Inkundla ya Bantu* noted that 'The Transkeian progressives have made a definite bid to win the support of this section of the population. They go into the homes and huts of the people; they sleep and eat and chat together with them and condition their mode of thinking in this intimate way.' Ruth First wrote later of Govan that, while he used official sources and statistics in his writings, 'the commoners of the Transkei were his chief source of information, and as he loved them, so they trusted and confided in him'.

4

Township politics

Ladysmith and Port Elizabeth, 1952–1960

Politically, Govan Mbeki's years in the Transkei ended in anti-climax, with the loss of his main base in the Transkei Organised Bodies. Financially, the struggle to keep the trading store profitable was sapped by other, even less successful ventures. Domestically, a troubled marriage reached breaking point. In 1952 Epainette confronted him, insisting initially that she leave Mbewuleni and find a teaching job, before agreeing that he leave and that she would stay on with the trading store and the four children.

And so in 1953 Govan left Idutywa and travelled to Ladysmith, Natal, to take up a teaching post. Two years later, in 1955, he moved to Port Elizabeth. More was involved than physical relocation. Mbeki's life was to be lived in a new register, following different rhythms. The shift from small-town Transkei to the port city meant that his political base was no longer rural but urban. His politics were no longer conducted in public or in 'respectable' organisations. He threw himself into sustained activism, operating largely under cover, a step or two ahead of the Special Branch. In 1953 he joined the new South African Communist Party (SACP), formed underground after the banning in 1950 of the old Communist Party, and his Party work saw his politics take on a tough, even unyielding, militancy. For Mbeki, the pen was always a favoured weapon. He wrote prolifically in these years, both for publication (including his best-known work, *The Peasants' Revolt)* and for clandestine circulation. This chapter traces the pattern of politics in Ladysmith and New Brighton, Port Elizabeth, until Sharpeville and the State of Emergency in 1960.

How land, people and politics go together: Mbeki in Ladysmith

Gillian Hart interviewed Govan on his sojourn in Ladysmith, and in her *Disabling Globalization* provides an important assessment of his political role and impact in the town and its rural periphery; and this account of Mbeki in Ladysmith draws on her work. His teaching post was in the high school in Steadville, the Ladysmith township, although he later taught as well in a school in Ephumakeni. As he had previously – at Taylor Street, Adams College and Clarkebury – he took his classroom duties seriously, but was equally zealous in extra-curricular instruction. Hart spoke to people in Ladysmith who were too young to have met Mbeki at the time, yet 'recall stories told by their elders of regular meetings that came to be known as "Oom Gov's university"'.

Mbeki's first political contacts in Ladysmith were Dr Achmad Sader and other Natal Indian Congress activists. He addressed Indian communities in Ladysmith, Dundee and Newcastle – 'we visited at night after school hours'. But he also forged links with Africans in Steadville and in two communities just north of Ladysmith, Driefontein and Ephumakeni – blocs of land held in freehold by *kholwa* African landholders. These families knew all too well that their properties were under jeopardy, that they were regarded as anomalies in terms of apartheid geography, and that white farmers were poised to occupy the land after their removal. At Ephumakeni (also known as Roosboom) and at Driefontein Mbeki was introduced to the leaders of local resistance to the removals. 'We talked,' recalled Govan. 'The question is what can we do?'

Talking to these hard-pressed rural people meant listening. A constant theme when others describe Govan's political interventions was his ability to hear, understand and respond to popular hopes and fears. In Ladysmith, his engagements changed the tone and tempo of local ANC politics. Elderly residents of the district stressed the value of his presence and told Gillian Hart 'how the meetings he organized generated tremendous intellectual ferment and excitement, and helped transform people's understandings of themselves, the conditions they confronted, and the possibilities for political action'. One veteran of the period told her that the ANC in the late 1940s and early 1950s had effectively excluded less educated people like himself: 'I was not very happy because we were told that meetings were run by educated people. Ordinary people like me were not allowed to join. There was that feeling that the movement belonged to the elite. [Things changed when] Mbeki was transferred here ... He was also our teacher. We had meetings with him, although this was not allowed in public ... we met regularly with him.'

Another Steadville resident said that Oom Gov had helped people understand how 'land, people, and politics go together'. When he was not working with the landholders, Govan also met with coal miners at Dannhauser and with residents of Steadville. Much of his work was directed towards the Congress of the People, eliciting grievances and demands from local people, which were sent to the group in Johannesburg drafting the Freedom Charter. The authorities were aware of some of these activities; and Govan savoured the memory of one way in which he managed to sidestep the police: 'I started a dancing school at the [Steadville] primary school ... There was a young lady who was teaching at the same school. She was pretty, she was attractive, she was my partner. In the afternoons we used to go there and attract a number of people – teachers and others who wanted to learn about ballroom dancing. I would slip out ... If security popped in, people were happily dancing ... in the course of dancing, she gave me coverage.'

But this charming subterfuge could only buy time. In April 1955 Govan was hardly surprised to receive a letter banning him from teaching. At about this time, he was approached by Fred Carneson and Ivan Schermbrucker, Communist Party members, and offered the post of local editor and office manager of the newspaper *New Age* in Port Elizabeth. (*New Age* was the title adopted when the Communist Party's paper, the *Guardian*, was banned in 1950.) And in July 1955 Govan slipped out of Natal and made his way to the port city. He entered a distinctive political setting, quite unlike either the rural Transkei or the Natal Midlands. Port Elizabeth was the cradle of organised African politics in South Africa; from the late 19th century to the 1930s an African middle class used the political space made available by a relatively liberal city administration. Central to their approach was the demand that 'civilised' Africans be extended full civil rights. But this mode of elite-led negotiating and supplication was shouldered aside in the 1940s by a more robust, more militant mass-based politics.

'It was rewarding work': clandestine political organisation in Port Elizabeth

New Brighton was the main African township, with a complex social geography. It comprised not only McNamee Village, built between 1938 and 1943 (and hailed by the City Council as a 'new model township'), but also the oldest section, Red Location, a squalid, crowded ghetto where most homes lacked basic services. By 1946 New Brighton was home to some 35,000 people. Further south lay Korsten, often described as a township for Coloureds – but the only area of the city where Africans had the right to freehold title, and home to thousands of Africans who moved to the city in the 1930s and 1940s, often renting crowded rooms from landlords across racial divides.

These townships generated a series of community protests in the 1940s, around bread-and-butter issues such as food and transport prices, rent increases and the imposition of lodgers' permits. These issues became closely bound up with strikes and protests mounted by a new form of trade unionism: a labour movement (as Janet Cherry puts it) 'much more directed by conscious political intentions'. Strikes were linked with political and community struggles. These new political energies were harnessed and led by younger, working-class activists: men and women such as Gladstone Tshume, Clifford Dladla, Caleb Mayekiso, Raymond Mhlaba, Adam Mati, Lily Diedericks and Frances Baard. Each of these individuals wore several organisational hats: the leadership of the unions, the Communist Party and the ANC overlapped and interpenetrated. While the ANC in other cities (notes Tom Lodge) was led by professional elites, 'in Port Elizabeth working-class leaders dominated African politics'. By 1944, the ANC's Secretary-General, the Rev. James Calata, wrote wearily from Cradock that 'influences of communism' were preventing any influence he had on Congress branches in Port Elizabeth.

In 1952 the Defiance Campaign was more successful in Port Elizabeth than anywhere else in the country, largely because it was preceded by eight years of popular protests. Township residents supported the national anti-pass campaign of 1944; rent boycotts in 1945 and 1951; the 1945–6 strike by dock-workers; the 1947 protests against food prices; the laundry workers' strike of 1948; and the bus boycott of 1949. The Defiance Campaign was initially a spectacular success in the city. Highly disciplined, trained volunteers submitted themselves for arrest after breaking apartheid restrictions. The first three months of the campaign saw 1,800 men and women arrested. Trade unions defended activists, calling lightning strikes when firms refused to employ volunteers. The membership of the New Brighton ANC branch grew from under 3,000 to 13,000 in a month, with eager recruits also in the Korsten and Dassieskraal branches. But on 18 October a minor incident at the North End railway station triggered a riot, during which four white men were killed by angry crowds, mostly of young men; private and public property was attacked; and seven Africans were shot by police. The events shook the City Council to its core, and it retreated from its erstwhile paternalism to a reluctant embrace of the full paraphernalia of influx control, curfews, bans on political meetings and scapegoating of activists.

This was the backdrop to the political stage Mbeki mounted in 1955. Any organised politics was doubly difficult: in 1953 the ANC was prohibited from holding meetings in New Brighton, and activism was a high risk for individuals. Following the Defiance Campaign, most of the senior members of the ANC in Port Elizabeth were banned, and 13 were charged with contravening the Suppression of Communism Act. Yet the mobilisation of thousands in the preceding decade could not simply be banished by state disapproval nor wished away by a nervy City Council. The challenge was for leaders to find new ways of engaging with an ardent mass base; and Mbeki was up to the challenge. In later years, he said it was precisely these testing conditions that whetted wiles and sharpened skills. In March 1956 the stakes were raised. A *Government Gazette* made it an offence for anyone to hold, preside at or address any gathering of ten Africans or more, in the districts of Port Elizabeth and Humansdorp. Normal politics were proscribed. The solution was to operate below the radar, to take activism underground. 'From '56 we were compelled to duck,' Govan told me. 'Now it was during this time, 1956 to 1960, that we perfected methods of working underground.'

But what form of politics did this mean? How was clandestine resistance to be waged? What rules governed the new game? As it happened, a sketchy draft set of rules was available in the shape of the M-Plan. This provided for an underground cell structure, so that leaders could communicate with each other and their followers. In Port Elizabeth, the *amaVolontiya*, veterans of the Defiance Campaign, were allocated to street committees. Each ANC member was responsible for monitoring ten houses. As Alvon Bennie told the SADET interviewer, 'That was my job for the whole year. In that house stays so-and-so who is a member of the ANC. In number so-and-so stays so-and-so who is a policeman ... As I am sitting here, I would be able to know the 10 houses here. And the next person knows the next 10 houses ... Then these streets were grouped into a zone. And we would report to a zone steward ... that was the system.'

Embryonic structures of this sort were established by the time Mbeki arrived in the city and plugged into an existing political circuit. His job in the *New Age* office put him in immediate contact with Communist Party comrades (who were also running ANC cells and trying to sustain the trade unions). As he recalled, 'by the time I had come here I had been given already the names of my contacts – Ray [Mhlaba], Gladstone Tshume, A.P. Mati, and so the moment I got here I got in touch with these people.'

Govan's key contribution to mobilisation in Port Elizabeth was essentially one of political education. He made an early decision. The Communist Party had been running study groups for workers for 15 years (Ray Mhlaba's memoirs attest to their importance in his political awareness) – but the ANC had no equivalent. 'So I said no, we should go further than that ... the people who are going to bear the brunt of the struggle are the members of the ANC. It is they who must understand why they are in the struggle, why they must suffer ...' He then mounted a programme of political education without equal in any South African city in the 1950s. He wrote, cyclostyled and distributed a booklet of about 50 pages, called *Isikhokhelo ngesimo nenkqubo ye ANC*, outlining the history, aims and policies of the movement. Govan was very clear that the booklet must be in Xhosa, accessible to a grassroots readership. (Others in the Party, like Fred Carneson, criticised this decision: 'they say: how can you talk Marxism in Xhosa? ... And my answer always was, surely the Chinese which have got the biggest Communist Party in the world, they don't teach them in English!') Govan also used a device for the book that he had encountered with Bible readings as a boy: specified portions of the text were to be read week by week.

The booklet was used by study groups, each of ten people, meeting in secret. There were eventually scores and scores of such groups. Taking steps to avoid the scrutiny of the police, or their informers, became Govan's everyday practice. Under conditions of illegality, he pointed out, 'we could not meet at our homes. I would get a notice say at the office or when I get home ... a little slip to say "corner such and such a street, such and such a time".' Govan had a well-deserved reputation for being very strict about punctuality – the last thing he wished was to be observed waiting at a street corner: 'If they are late, you leave.' In an interview with Bridget Thompson, Govan reflected on this *modus operandi*: 'in fact I think I'm happier with underground work. For so many years we were doing underground work and I became happy there ... You work deep into the night. Addressing, discussing problems in small groups in the townships. Often I used to leave work at 5 o'clock, I'll get back in the townships, have a cup of coffee, and then get buried in the townships in these small political classes. I'll be back home between 12 and 1 a.m. Only then to have my supper. But it was rewarding work. It was rewarding work. Because from those small classes we got people who became trained ... And they would go out in turn to do what you are doing with them.'

If each in a group reached this level, and taught ten others, 'then you quickly got to a hundred – it snowballed like that.' Political education was one underground activity; another was the production of leaflets for distribution across the townships. Govan considered the leaflet 'a great instrument in the hands of a revolutionary who's been working under conditions of illegality'. It would be pushed through thousands of doors: 'And every home reads the leaflet and they keep talking about it in every home.' He warmed to the theme. Leaflets were better than speeches made at a rally: as soon as people left the venue, the spoken word 'goes with the wind. A leaflet, a written word, goes into every home. And it would be talked about for a long time. It's exciting, underground work ... It is very, very rewarding.'

The cumulative sense of the years between 1953 and 1963 is of a life intensely lived – yet also a life narrowed, pared down to political commitment, permitting little beyond. One gets a sense of the intensity, but also of its cost, from the memories of those who knew him at the time. Govan was close to Sonya and Brian Bunting, both Party members and both involved in producing *New Age*. (At one point, he arranged for his daughter, Linda, to stay with the Buntings in Cape Town, so that she might mix with white South Africans who were not racists.) Brian Bunting, asked how he remembered Govan during the *New Age* years, was admiring: 'My memory of Govan at that period was a very tall, commanding and decisive presence. A sort of combination of power and influence. He has a very impressive personality and I was always astonished by the sort of communication he had on the one hand with the African rank and file – his common touch, as it were – and at the same time the ease with which he would get on with sophisticated white academics.'

Sonya recalled him as 'a tower of strength' in New Brighton politics, tireless in his commitment. She then added, 'I think he was a very strong, determined individual, you know, who put everything after his political commitments and responsibilities. I really do think that.' His friendships were defined by his politics. Mary Benson recalled that Govan was initially disinclined to meet Christopher Gell, because he thought him a Liberal. When they did meet, Govan found the remarkable Gell – journalist and campaigner, confined for most hours to an iron lung – 'very fine' and they spent many hours together discussing ideas. Ruth First noted that Govan could be a 'stern disciplinarian'; that he had a sharp mind 'intolerant of the foolish and faint-hearted'. Brian Bunting told me an anecdote that chimes with this judgement. He met the young Joe Matthews for the first time in the *New Age* office in Port Elizabeth, and was 'held enthralled' for two hours. 'After he had gone (he was a very young chap at that time) I said to Govan, "A bright boy!" "Well," said Govan, "he's a gas bag – he talks and does nothing. If there's a job to do you won't find him."'

Hilda and Rusty Bernstein responded to researchers from the University of Amsterdam on the occasion of Govan's honorary doctorate in 1977. Hilda said: 'Govan by no means fits the classic image of a revolutionary ... He is not an agitator but someone who quietly – there is no better way of putting it –

manages to convince his opponent by argument. If you met him somewhere during a meeting of a congress, he always gave the impression that he was very timid, but in fact he has immense political passions and a will of iron.' Rusty agreed. Govan had retained too much of the teacher's character ever to be aggressive or violent. 'Convincing people, explaining patiently all sorts of things, that was much more like Govan, but once he is convinced of a certain course of action, it is very difficult to change his mind. Some people found him rigid at times, but once the discussion was over he was as pleasant and sympathetic as always.'

One final glimpse of Govan during the 1950s reinforces the sense of one who 'put everything behind his political commitments', and adds a layer of domestic poignancy. Moeletsi Mbeki, who would have been in his teens at the time, remembered his father returning from Port Elizabeth to Idutywa at weekends 'when the political situation permitted'. The shop 'was an important link in the distribution of *New Age* … My father spent most of his weekends working on articles.'

5

Mbeki as journalist and author, 1955–1963

This chapter moves from political education classes in township kitchens to political education through the printed word. Mbeki worked for *New Age*: he ran the office, wrote articles and took photographs, and mailed copy to Cape Town where the paper was printed. He lived in New Brighton, from 1956 or 1957 staying with his kinswoman, in Ferguson Street. The *New Age* office was in the city centre, in the Court Chambers building, opposite the main law court. His colleagues were Nondwe Mankahla, James Kati and Mountain Ngqungwana – although (said Govan) the last-mentioned 'really worked for the Party, he was a Party employee; but according to the … documents he was employed by the *New Age*'. Govan filed scores of stories over his years with the paper.

His first by-line, in August 1955, was a story

headlined 'In the Valley Where Death Stalks', covering a typhoid outbreak in the Sundays River valley orange orchards. Mbeki deftly contrasted the local farmers (with 'big American cars', dominating the pavements or lounging in restaurants) with their impoverished workforce. He outlined the political economy of the valley with details of prices, rents and wages of the stricken labourers' families, but concluded with an optimistic paragraph. In this 'valley of despair' six ANC branches had been established. People had lost hope, 'but when the message of the struggle … reached them, they seized on it with a faith that borders on religion … When there is hope there is a way.'

Govan submitted stories on events in Port Elizabeth and on surrounding farms ('Thousands Hear Lilian Ngoyi in PE'; 'This Is Site and Service – Women and Children Sleep in the Open'; 'The Farmers Still Want Slaves'; 'Port Elizabeth Workers Join Bus Boycott', 'PE Boycott Gathers Momentum'; 'PE Turned into Armed Camp') and also on the Ciskei and Transkei: 'Famine Menaces Reserves'; 'Ciskei and Transkei Famine Is Unbroken'; 'Transkei Chief [K.D. Matanzima] Shouted Down'; and a fascinating story in September 1957 headed 'There IS Unrest in the Transkei, but It Is Not Caused by Moscow-Trained Saboteurs'.

The story recounted rumours swirling through the white community in the Transkei – unidentified submarines off the Pondoland coast; strange lights at night; peasants wading through the surf to board a Soviet vessel for training – and asked, 'Are the Transkei traders seeing ghosts?' Yes, discontent was rife. 'But it is born of the intolerable economic conditions which are turning the whole area into one vast refugee paupers' camp.' The article then described acute struggles being waged over land, cattle, fences, and increasingly coercive regulations. Peasant communities had hired lawyers to resist evictions, but they also tore down unwanted fences, attacked unpopular headmen, and held meetings to oppose the introduction of the apartheid system of Bantu Authorities. 'If the peasants' peaceful innocence in Verwoerd's largest make-believe colony is disturbed, it is the Nats and their apartheid laws who are the saboteurs.'

Another Transkei story ran in January 1959 under the heading 'The People Are Dying – Land, Stock Taken from Transkei Peasants'. Drawing on a recent trip to the Transkei and interviews with local people, Mbeki detailed the powers that the Bantu Authorities Act conferred on 'a ruling aristocracy of corrupt appointed chiefs'. Peasants resented the new taxes, especially the 10s General Levy, which they called *Impundulu* – the blood-sucking bird of Xhosa legend. Public meetings were banned unless convened by one of the 'large army of Bantu Authorities officials', whose praises would be sung by a 'soulless stooge' to hasten the closing of the meeting.

In addition to his coverage for *New Age*, Govan also wrote during the 1950s for two other left-wing publications, *Fighting Talk* and *Liberation*. The first was the mouthpiece of the Congress of Democrats and, under Ruth First's editorship, appeared monthly until its banning in 1962. *Liberation* ('a journal of democratic discussion') was edited by Michael Harmel, the Communist Party theoretician, and covered international and local issues, as well as more theoretical pieces. The Bantu Authorities Act of 1951 was central to the National Party's plans for 'separate development'. It sought to create several tiers of local authorities in the Reserves, in order to restore the standing and authority of local chiefs and minimise popular participation in decision-making. The Act was not implemented in any Reserve area until in 1955 the Transkeian Territories General Council – or *Bhunga* – was cajoled into voting itself out of existence in favour of a new Territorial Authority. This was formalised by Proclamation 180 of 1956 – and triggered Mbeki's engagement with the issue.

Mbeki recognised the significance of the Bantu Authorities approach. 'Now I decided to work on that. Now every Sunday I would go to the office, I would lock myself up there and hide.' He 'hid' in order to do the research, scouring press reports, official documents and the Blue Books emanating from the *Bhunga* in Umtata. He sent the fruit of these labours to Brian Bunting for serialisation in *New Age*, but Bunting recommended that a study of that length should rather appear in *Liberation*. And between September 1956 and April 1957, Govan's analysis of the implications of the Bantu Authorities Act appeared in four parts as 'The Transkei Tragedy'. He was of course resuming analysis of a region that he had commenced 20 years earlier, with *Transkei in the Making*. But the *Liberation* series was more trenchant, more politically combative, than the earlier work.

He hammered away at themes that he had raised for 20 years: that the fundamental economic problem of the Transkei was the shortage of land; that the poverty created by landlessness suited the needs of the mines and other employers; that long-term labour migrancy took a cruel toll on family life and social cohesion; and that chiefs (now restyled as Bantu Authorities) must carry out a land policy which peasants had already strongly opposed. Chiefs would now remove families under betterment schemes and dispossess others in the name of soil conservation; keep the landless in labour camps; and compel people to cull their cattle, build roads, eradicate weeds – and they would have new coercive powers to carry out this agenda. In a passage that anticipated subsequent scholarship, Mbeki traced continuities in policy from the Glen Grey Act (1894), the Native Administration Act (1927), the Hertzog laws of 1936, the Rehabilitation Scheme of the 1940s and the Bantu Authorities: 'The latest in this series of "schemes" to solve the desperate needs of a land-hungry people without giving them land.'

A prescient passage warned that, as popular dissatisfaction grew, 'it is the Bantu Authority who will appeal to the Nationalists to bring in armed police to crush the dissatisfaction' and that as men and women emerged as leaders of popular resistance 'the Bantu Authority will appeal to the Nationalists to deport them as "agitators" and "communists"'. However, the Nationalists should learn from history: as the fate of 'the Pharaohs, the Hitlers, the Mussolinis' showed, 'history is on the side of the people'. The series concluded by suggesting that Verwoerd's department should not too hastily congratulate itself on the fact that the *Bhunga* had accepted the Bantu Authorities scheme. 'The Bunga had no mandate to speak, and it did not speak, on behalf of the people. The last word lies with the people, and they have not spoken yet.'

The series recalled earlier forms of popular resistance to attempts by the state to control and refashion the Reserves, and accorded 'the last word' to such resistance in the future. In an article in

Fighting Talk, published in May 1958, Govan took this theme further in a section headed 'Growing Peasant Resistance'. The government had 'eliminated the influence of the teacher on the rural African's public life' and had dragooned chiefs into serving as their agents, so 'the simple peasant had no choice but to turn to his own class for leadership and face the Nationalist threat to his existence. The peasant has resisted bitterly the "betterment schemes", the mass removals from homes ... they have resisted the culling of their stock ... [and the extension of pass laws to women]. It takes a long time to arouse the peasant to any form of resistance against established authority. But as his conservatism may be a stumbling block to the growth of progressive ideas, so it too can also hold up the plans of a government that must first destroy the established order of the peasant to carry out its plans of economic enslavement under the apartheid dream.'

It is a striking passage, not only for its heterodoxy in terms of conventional Marxist analyses in South Africa at the time, but also for the way it presages his best-known published work, *The Peasants' Revolt*. Despite its title, only one chapter of *The Peasants' Revolt* – 23 out of 148 pages – deals directly with the peasant resistance in Mpondoland, and in fact its first draft was completed before the Mpondo revolt began.

Govan originally set out to write a manual for ANC organisers, outlining what was taking place in the Reserves. In the course of researching and writing it, it grew into what he and his collaborator Ruth First called 'the book on Bantustans'. Its first five chapters provide an overview history of the evolution of policies for administering the 'Native Reserves': from Shepstone in Natal and the Cape governments in the 19th century, to Rhodes and the Glen Grey Act and the establishment of the Council system and *Bhunga* in the Transkei, to the introduction of Bantu Authorities and (in a chapter that revisits the *Liberation* analysis) the fateful decision by the *Bhunga* to buy into the Verwoerdian project.

The sixth chapter, titled 'Peasants in Poverty', forcefully restates Mbeki's earlier writings on the Reserves as labour reservoirs, the rise of a class of landless people, and dwindling productivity. 'The essential problem of the reserves has always been – as it still is – too many people on too little land.' The result could be seen in the Ciskei, 'with its ravaged earth and sunken peasantry', outcome of a policy 'inspired by the insatiable appetite for more and more labour on the reserves'. Chapter 8, 'Chiefs in the Saddle', breaks new ground in Mbeki's writings on the Transkei. It provides a vivid picture of local struggles between chiefs and commoners, in the new legal context provided by Bantu Authorities status. Mbeki draws attention to the 'stubborn resistance' and 'uncompromising opposition of the peasants' against rehabilitation measures, and the use by the chiefs of the 'Bush Courts' or Bantu Authorities Tribunals. Mbeki is unsparing in his critique of the chiefs, 'the new jockeys riding the reserve horse, who have applied the spurs'. The chiefs were pivotal to the Bantustan scheme. They constituted 'a ruling aristocracy, but one directly answerable to the government. The Chiefs are Chiefs because the government has ordained that they may be so.' They were vested with greater powers than they had ever had since colonial conquest, but were 'expected to use their powers to keep quiescent not only the great mass of the dispossessed Africans … but the landholders and small middle class as well.'

Chapter 9, 'Resistance and Rebellion: The Peasants Rise' was written in dramatic circumstances and provided what for 20 years was the fullest account of the Mpondo revolt. It drew on press reports, Hansard and the *Government Gazette*, and the memorandum sent by the Intaba (Mountain) Committee to the United Nations, but its details and sense of atmosphere were based on Govan's own meetings with the Mpondo rebels and especially with Anderson Ganyile. It recounts the events from March 1960 – when overt resistance flared in Bizana district – through the Ngquza massacre on 6 June to the State of Emergency imposed in November 1960, the incarceration of 5,000 people and the trials of over 2,000 men and women involved in the revolt. The chapter emphasised the extent of organisation achieved in Eastern Mpondoland; how local grievances were linked to broader objectives ('people soon realized that they had a common enemy in the government and the Chiefs'); the discipline of the activists, and their tactical repertoire.

There is no doubt whatsoever of the significance of these events for Mbeki the activist. After Sharpeville, urban resistance was snuffed out by army and police within weeks: 'Yet in Pondoland … resistance, far from abating, spread not only from village to village, but also in neighbouring districts, increasing all the while in intensity. It was in these reserve areas, too, that the struggle assumed the truly mass character which it lacked elsewhere … The march through Bizana, when an old man carrying a black flag at half-mast led a procession of 5,000 peasants without any experience of mass forms of pressure, must be one of the greatest feats of organizational ability that the liberation movement and the oppressed people of this country have so far accomplished.'

Admiration for what the Mpondo rebels achieved was of course also vindication of Mbeki's own, long-held belief that the ANC should pay more attention to the Reserves; that peasant resistance had a place to play in the struggle for national liberation. It presented (he said) 'the first real proof that the ANC should focus on mobilisation of *both* city and rural dwellers – an argument I had been putting forward since the 1930s'. Where he had failed to convince his colleagues, the Mpondo rebels did so by example. Their rising 'had a resounding impact on the thinking of the Congress leadership'. 'The leaders realized at last that a struggle based on the reserves had a much greater capacity to absorb the shocks of government repression [than those based on urban locations] ... The struggles of the peasants start from smaller beginnings, build up to a crescendo over a much longer time ... A proper blending of the peasant and worker struggles, therefore, coupled with skilful timing of joint action, is a matter that must engage the serious thinking of the leadership.'

In addition to his sustained intellectual engagement with developments in the Transkei, and his attention to forms of peasant resistance, Mbeki during his Port Elizabeth years sought through political practice to link rural and urban struggles. He did so in several ways. Firstly, he travelled frequently to rural areas, in the Ciskei and in the Transkei. The contacts that have received most attention were two trips to Mpondoland

Govan wrote most of the text during 1958 and 1959, secreting draft chapters as they were completed. When he was detained in solitary confinement after his arrest in 1962, Govan rewrote parts of the book from memory – and drafted a chapter on the Mpondo revolt. He had given up smoking, but spent the cash he had on tobacco, which he then traded with white convicts for sheets of toilet paper. These were hidden in a copy of *Oliver Twist* and smuggled out to a typist. After his acquittal, two manuscripts existed: that completed in 1960, and the second, written before and during detention. At this point (wrote Ruth First) she worked to reconcile the two versions and edit the manuscript into final form. They both worked again on the text in early 1963. Then came the Rivonia raid and First's '117 days' in detention. But by then the book was in other hands – identified by First only as 'friends in Cape Town', but in fact Ray Alexander and Jack Simons. They checked quotations and added references and rewrote parts of some chapters – and finally sent the text to Ruth in London.

once the revolt there had begun; but he also held meetings in Peddie, Middledrift, Tsomo, Lady Frere, Cala and other centres. Govan's first contact with the Mpondo resisters was agreed by the Party leadership in Port Elizabeth, despite Mhlaba's scepticism ('I felt that the revolt was doomed and wanted it to end'). Govan and his friend Tolly Bennun wanted to respond to the approach the rebels had made. Bennun owned a leather factory in Uitenhage – an unlikely calling, but excellent cover for an active underground Communist and subsequently MK technician. The pair travelled with Govan driving, in a chauffeur's white coat, and Bennun seated in the rear: a colour-coded disguise that turned racial stereotyping to an advantage. Govan's key contact in Pondoland was the young Anderson Ganyile, a protégé. He made a second visit, also in 1960, and met Mpondo resisters in Durban as well.

Secondly, Govan made a particular point of organising within the migrant single quarters, contacting migrant workers who historically had little to do with urban politics. Migrant workers were housed in hostels, called *Oondokwenza* locally, and Mbeki was proud of the underground links set up with the sector: 'we did something here that had not been done anywhere else'. Single-quarter housing was normally allocated to men who came from the same rural locations. They knew each other, which facilitated the creation of structures and practices for taking collective decisions, and for raising and saving funds. The ANC recognised these informal structures and hierarchies and used them as points of entry to the hostels. Once trust was established, Mbeki and others would select individuals, and provide them with intensive political tuition. They would then serve as emissaries to the countryside, introducing urban activists to key local figures, providing them with safe houses. 'Again, it was this connection, rural *and* urban,' Govan emphasised. Migrants recruited in this way proved crucial after Sharpeville, when the ANC was operating entirely underground. Andrew Masondo told Sifiso Ndlovu, in an interview, how he became a rural area organiser: 'I worked in the Rural Area Organisers' cell under Govan. I worked with Vuyisile Mini, James Kati, Mayekiso, and Mkhabela ... We, the Eastern Cape, developed a very good way of organising the rural areas', shuttling between city and countryside along a circuit of known sympathisers.

Thirdly, Mbeki was particularly keen to ensure that his favoured weapon – the underground leaflet – was distributed as widely as possible in the Ciskei and Transkei. Production of these was centralised and made more efficient. Individual branches in Port Elizabeth were advised to jettison their typewriters and duplicators: too many in operation was a security risk. Instead, Govan and Mountain Ngqungwana took on the task of producing leaflets for the city and its rural hinterland. Mbeki wrote the leaflets; Ngqungwana would type the stencil in one part of the city and take it from there to be duplicated elsewhere. By 1960, Mbeki was also producing a monthly broadsheet specifically intended for rural districts, called *Izwe Lomzi* (The Voice of the People). Jock Strachan – in his wry memoir of his days as an underground operative in Port Elizabeth – was responsible for cyclostyling thousands of copies of *Izwe Lomzi* in a safe house in Walmer. Under a table sound-proofed with mattresses, two Gestetner cyclostyle printers ran 'non-stop, week after week', and the printed wads of the paper were delivered by car: 'at a certain mileage along a certain road would appear an uncertain motor car with uncertain number plates ... its boot open ... at ten p.m. precisely, and I mean absolutely precisely.' The printed paper was loaded into the parked car, and the stencil for the next issue retrieved. 'To this day, as far as I know,' remarks Strachan, 'nobody ever found out where the broadsheets were coming from, and we had the paper going for more than six months.'

Mention of Ganyile and Ngqungwana is relevant to another lasting contribution made by Govan Mbeki to resistance politics in South Africa: his role as recruiter, mentor and formative influence on scores of younger comrades. Ngqungwana was probably the pseudonymous author of an affectionate portrait of Govan in *African Communist*. It recounted how Youth Leaguers at Fort Hare in the 1950s were particularly struck by the fact that 'even our great "guns" in the academic circles … like Prof. Z.K. Matthews, had talked with very high esteem of this "Gov"'. After the State of Emergency in 1960 had been lifted, 'finally, one New Brighton Sunday morning – it happened. A tallish, clean, grey-trousered and light-green-jacketed figure … came walking up Mendi Road.' A few days later, he was one of the students who were invited to meet Mbeki. 'And immediately we were reminded about discipline, including "not to come a minute earlier or later than the set time".' The article recalled the lecture delivered by Govan 'in that badly lit, specially arranged small bedroom'; and how a concern about security was taken to their new teacher. They were overwhelmed to learn 'that he knew the personal life and problems of each and every one of us' and had made his own decision as to the trustworthiness of the man under suspicion.

The New Brighton study circles provided recruits who followed Govan into the underground, into MK, and onto Robben Island: the likes of Henry Fazzie, Edgar Ngoyi and Vuyisile Mini (executed in 1964) all identified Mbeki as a mentor and guide. Fort Hare campus also provided Govan with cadres who became struggle icons in their own right – and who retained a near reverence for the man under whose tutelage they cut their political teeth. Chris Hani was one of these: recruited into the Communist Party while he was still a student. Zola Skweyiya was another. So was Andrew Masondo. Offered a lectureship at Fort Hare in 1960, and unsure whether to accept it, he turned to Govan for advice. 'He was my chief.'

6

The road to Rivonia

Between March 1960 and July 1963 – from Sharpeville to the Rivonia raid – Govan's life changed decisively. Detained under the State of Emergency, he played a key role in the decision to turn to armed struggle (and was party to long-running controversy over its form); he was a founder member of Umkhonto weSizwe (henceforth MK); ran a sabotage cell in Port Elizabeth; was arrested, charged and acquitted; chaired the ANC's first exiled conference; went underground; and was rounded up when police swooped on Lilliesleaf farm.

On 21 March 1960, Govan Mbeki – in chauffeur's livery – was driving Tolly Bennun's big Buick through the Transkei. The previous day, Mbeki – by then *persona non grata* with Kaiser Matanzima's Bantustan administration – had met clandestinely with activists in Cala district. Somewhere between Umtata and Durban the men heard a radio bulletin on the shootings at Sharpeville. At the *New Age* office in Durban, there was a message asking Govan to phone Oliver Tambo; he did so, and was urged to attend an emergency meeting of the ANC's National Executive Committee in Johannesburg. He and Bennun drove there the following day, and that evening the available members of the NEC met in Orlando East.

The meeting must have been conducted in a blur of confusion, uncertainty and tension. Yet those present made weighty decisions with long-term consequences. The plan that Tambo should leave the country to win support overseas was brought forward. There would be a Day of Mourning on 28 March. Crucially – anticipating that the ANC might be banned – it was agreed that in the event the organisation should continue to operate, illegally. And to make that new mode of existence more feasible, the cumbersome structures of the ANC would be streamlined to just three tiers of leadership, with seven members appointed by the NEC at national, regional and branch levels.

The massacre at Sharpeville was followed by what Tom Lodge has called 'a popular insurrection' in Cape Town's townships, and by confrontations and violence in other cities. The state responded swiftly. On Wednesday 30 March a State of Emergency was declared, and that night nearly 2,000 political activists were arrested across the country and detained (that number rose to almost 10,000 by mid-May). By 8 April, the government had rushed through its Unlawful Organisations Act, and both the Pan Africanist Congress (PAC) and the ANC were banned. Mbeki, Mhlaba and other Port Elizabeth activists were held in Rooi Hel (as North End Prison was widely known). Conditions were appalling: the prison could not cope with the influx of detainees from Cradock, Grahamstown and elsewhere in the Eastern Cape; men were crammed together in three cells (so overcrowded, said Govan, 'that no one was able to lie on his back'), their bedding infested with lice, food – bitter *pap* – served in tin cans, the warders jumpy and hostile.

This was Govan's first extended stay in prison. He was released only on 31 August, when the State of Emergency ended. A vivid sense of his five months in Rooi Hel is available in the diary he kept, and subsequently passed on to Mary Benson. She read excerpts when she gave evidence to the United Nations Committee on Apartheid in March 1964: 'Perhaps if I quote from it you will see another side to this disciplined and dedicated man.'

Out of detention, Mbeki immediately immersed himself in the familiar mix of journalism, pamphleteering and underground networks. In

GOVAN MBEKI'S PRISON DIARY, AS RECORDED
BY MARY BENSON

He wrote with compassion about one old man in the cell, so rheumatic that his limbs swelled, yet never complaining nor using it as an excuse to try for release. Another prisoner who constantly prayed amused Mbeki, who observed that the prayers resembled the demands of workers to their employers for better conditions ... Of others again, Mbeki wrote: *'Every afternoon, we heard beatings from prisoners returning from work. Sometimes they would bellow. We heard the splattering of leather belts as they fell on a body. It is intolerable to listen and one shudders to think what effect this type of treatment must have on those who administer it as well as on the recipients. In the long run it is difficult to see how both can escape being turned into beasts.'*

... Yet the diary recorded other facets of their lives as well. They sang freedom songs and had daily discussions on a remarkably catholic range of subjects: the pass system; music; marriage; Afrikaner Nationalism; sex education; should ancient customs and relations be restored after freedom? – a lively discussion revealing that apart from the few on the far left, the majority regarded the restoration of customs as essential. When they discussed leadership, the essential qualities, they agreed, were *'personality, dignity, alertness, knowledge, intelligence, sincerity, perseverance, determination, restraint and humility.'* ... There were good moments: *'the knowledge that our own men abroad, such as Bishop Reeves and Oliver Tambo and others were sparing nothing of themselves to show up the brutality of this philosophy of racial supremacy.'* ... Mbeki commented that Defence and Aid Committees under the presidency of the Archbishop of Cape Town – distributing food and warm clothing to the detained – *'sealed bonds of friendship between the Africans and that section of the white population which realizes that the narrow racial nationalism of the NP cannot work in the world of today.'* Exuberantly he recorded the Trinidad dockers' refusal to handle South African goods.

*

December 1960 he attended two meetings. One was a Consultative Conference held in Orlando, attended not only by some three dozen Africans drawn from the ANC and PAC, but also Jordan Ngubane of the Liberal Party, and a scattering of ministers, businessmen and leaders of cultural and sporting groups. The main resolutions adopted called for an 'All-in conference representative of the African People', and endorsed 'effective use of non-violent pressures against apartheid' and 'a non-racial democracy'. The other meeting was held in secret, in Johannesburg, and involved about 20 members of the Communist Party. By Ben Turok's account, it was at this gathering that a formal decision was taken, accepting that a new phase of struggle was necessary. In response to state violence, it was necessary 'to create an armed force since the old ways of struggle were now so circumscribed'.

Even if this occasion marked a relatively formal decision in favour of armed struggle, it was not the first time that the shift was canvassed in Party circles. In July 1960 the Party had won a promise from China that training would be available for putative guerrilla soldiers. In August Michael Harmel wrote a paper, title borrowed from Lenin: 'What Is to Be Done?' – answering that the state had created a new situation 'leading inexorably to violence'. Others had contemplated a departure from non-violence even earlier. Several were from the Eastern Cape. Raymond Mhlaba advocated armed struggle as early as 1958 – although he acknowledges it was a minority position at the time. Andrew Masondo recounted that youth circles grew impatient with non-violence before 1960, and 'a group of us at Fort Hare actually formed a group to prepare for the eventuality of an armed struggle taking place'. Joe Matthews recalled that literature on Communist-led guerrilla struggles circulated in Port Elizabeth. When I asked Govan Mbeki about the significance of China, Vietnam and Cuba, he replied that 'the struggles in those countries had been studied and studied very, very closely'. For all of them – Govan in particular – predilection towards armed resistance was confirmed by events in Sekhukhuneland, Natal and Pondoland. Ruth First later wrote that Mbeki was 'one of the most important advocates of waging an armed struggle'.

The turn to armed struggle did not arise from any particular resolution, or any specific moment. It was drift rather than decision; a tumbleweed turning upon itself, buffeted by circumstances, gathering momentum. Although the details remain hazy, and disputed by some of those involved, it appears that the policy shift was first approved by the Party – which had, of course, been operating clandestinely since 1950 – and formally by the ANC only in June 1961.

But both bodies were reactive, feeling their way, flying by the seat of their pants. What they agreed on was the form of struggle: a programme of sabotage on selected targets, designed to avoid any casualties; carried out by members recruited to a new structure, nominally independent and staffed by militants across racial divides. The leadership of the new body was vested in a national High Command, with a Regional Command in each of Johannesburg, Durban, Cape Town and Port Elizabeth. By late 1961 there were perhaps 250 MK recruits, organised into units of three to four members. The first generation of MK combatants was high on courage, commitment and bravado. It was desperately short of training, relevant skills and appropriate materiel.

The first explosions took place on 16 December 1961. Port Elizabeth had become a centre of (relative) expertise: Jock Strachan and Tolly Bennun dredged up memories of chemistry, and devised timing devices, fuses and explosives. But one of their operatives was clumsy, and captured; two weeks later, Mbeki, Strachan and Joseph Jack were arrested and charged with offences under the Explosives Act. Govan spent five months in custody, three in solitary confinement. He staved off boredom by practising all the dance steps that he could recall; by playing tiddlywinks with maize seeds and an empty cup; by dredging up English and Latin verse – and by drafting what became the second version of *The Peasants' Revolt* on scraps of toilet paper obtained by barter. He went on trial, in effective for running a sabotage cell, and in an unlikely outcome was discharged. One of two witnesses due to testify against him bolted, and the other changed his story.

It was the second half of 1962. Govan filed his final stories for *New Age* before it was banned in September. That month, his comrade Ray Mhlaba was one of the first MK men sent to China for military training. Mbeki was busy recruiting new, young members of MK; arranging their passage out of the country for training; and fretting over their political readiness. It was still September when he left Port Elizabeth for Johannesburg, charged by the underground ANC to train up potential replacements for the NEC as bannings, house arrests and flight depleted capacities. In October, he made his way to Lobatse in Bechuanaland, where he chaired a meeting of the ANC – either its last organised conference before Morogoro in 1969, or an ad hoc scramble of available members, according to competing subsequent versions. In November 1962 he was served in Johannesburg with an order of house arrest, confining him to his home in New Brighton. He had stayed briefly with the trade unionist Dan Tloome and, when the police caught up with him, was staying, *sub rosa*, with Mary Moodley in Naledi, Johannesburg. But 'that same evening I was driven to Lilliesleaf farm'. Govan spent most of the next six months underground at Lilliesleaf – the property bought by the Communist Party in peri-urban Rivonia, which had served as Mandela's base prior to his arrest in August 1962.

Rusty Bernstein's *Memory Against Forgetting* has a chapter on 1962–3 aptly titled 'Things Fall Apart'. It conveys more persuasively than any other source just how ad hoc, makeshift and complacent the underground operatives of the ANC, Party and MK had become. By early 1963, Govan Mbeki personified the overlap between the three structures. Mandela was in prison; Sisulu was under house arrest; and Tambo was in London. Govan was now *de facto* the senior ANC leader at large. He was also a member of the SACP Central Committee; a founder member of MK, and a member of its High Command. No matter how hard he tried to adhere to the codes of clandestine operations that had served him well in Port Elizabeth, his various leadership roles rendered him trebly vulnerable. And it was becoming objectively more difficult to maintain discipline and coherence in makeshift underground structures. The apartheid state could now hold people for 90 days, in solitary confinement. The Special Branch applied forms of torture learned directly from France and the United States: people cracked under this pressure, and talked. House arrests immobilised some and drove others into exile. Lines of command and decision-making structures crumpled.

It was difficult to know who was wearing what hat, with what authority, and almost impossible to control comings and goings. From being a well-secured safe house, the Lilliesleaf farm became in effect the headquarters of MK, visited by an increasing number of people. Just when security should have become tighter, it became more porous. The underground movement now acquired a second property, Trevallyn, intended to become the base of MK. By early July, Mbeki, Mhlaba and Sisulu had moved from Lilliesleaf to Trevallyn. A meeting was called, to discuss Operation Mayibuye – but where would it take place? Govan and the other MK leaders insisted that security at Trevallyn should not be compromised. 'So it was decided, alright, let this be the very, very last meeting that takes place at Rivonia.' The meeting took place, on 11 July, at Lilliesleaf, despite considerable apprehension. Kathy Kathrada says that as the meeting approached, 'I became agitated and afraid.' Rusty Bernstein initially refused to attend, and yielded reluctantly, based on the condition that this should be the last time they gathered at the farm.

It was indeed the last time.

At three o'clock that afternoon police swarmed over the property. Apparently they were acting upon a tip-off that Sisulu would be there; but to their incredulous delight they arrested no fewer than 17 people, and carried off a treasure trove of documents. Bernstein and Bob Hepple, locked in the police van for several hours, 'could hear policemen … shouting to each other in excitement. "Look at this!" and "Jesus! Look what's here!"' Rivonia was a disaster. It decapitated the underground leadership, and, in the months that followed, the state was able to close in, too, on local remnants of MK and ANC cells. Karis and Gerhart note that an exiled leader, on hearing the news of the Rivonia raid, dubbed it 'the death knell of amateurism'. The judgement may sound harsh, but was undeniably accurate.

And no wonder Lieutenant Van Wyk and his men were excited. The papers they seized that day served as exhibits in the Rivonia trial; the most important by far was a document headed 'Operation Mayibuye'. It was written by Joe Slovo and Govan Mbeki (although this was not disclosed at the Rivonia trial).* 'Operation Mayibuye' remains one of the most contentious products of the struggle. Firstly, its viability is

* Several sources suggest that Arthur Goldreich may also have had a hand in its first version.

115

disputed. It envisioned organised groups of guerrillas, operating in rural areas, detonating broader struggles, leading eventually to protracted military operations against the apartheid regime. When it was first presented to the underground leadership, some found it inspirational; but its critics deemed it romantic and unrealistic. Secondly, ever since 1963 arguments have been waged as to its status and authority. Some (including Slovo, Mhlaba and Mbeki) insisted to the ends of their lives that 'Operation Mayibuye' had been approved by MK, the ANC and the Party, and had been sent to Tambo in exile on this basis. Others (like Mandela, Sisulu and Kathrada) insisted at the time, and subsequently, that the proposals were in draft form; had not been approved; and remained under consultation, inside and outside the country.

This latter version was presented by the defence during the Rivonia trial; and crucially so. At the outset, Percy Yutar for the prosecution called 'Operation Mayibuye' the 'corner-stone of the state case', alleging that when the defendants were arrested they were already organising armed insurrection. But Mr Justice Quartus de Wet interrupted Yutar during his closing address: did he concede that he 'had failed to prove guerrilla warfare was ever decided upon'? This judicial intervention removed the capstone of the prosecution case – 'As Your Lordship pleases,'

... It can now truly be said that very little, if any, scope exists for the smashing of white supremacy other than by means of mass revolutionary action, the main content of which is armed resistance leading to victory by military means. The political events which have occurred in the last few years have convinced the overwhelming majority of the people that no mass struggle which is not backed up by armed resistance and military offensive operations, can hope to make a real impact ...

The objective military conditions in which the movement finds itself makes the possibility of a general uprising leading to direct military struggle an unlikely one. Rather, as in Cuba, the general uprising must be sparked off by organised and well prepared guerrilla operations during the course of which the masses of the people will be drawn in and armed ...

The absence of friendly borders and long scale impregnable natural bases from which to operate are both disadvantages. But more important than these factors is the support of

> the people who in certain situations are better
> protection than mountains and forests. In the
> rural areas which become the main theatre
> of guerrilla operations ... the overwhelming
> majority of the people will protect and
> safeguard the guerrillas ...
>
> The following plan envisages a process
> which will place in the field ... armed and
> trained guerrilla bands who will find [others?]
> ready to join the local guerrilla bands with
> arms and equipment at their disposal ... In the
> initial period ... the cornerstone of guerrilla
> operations is 'shamelessly attack the weak and
> shamelessly flee from the strong' ...
>
> We are convinced that this plan is capable
> of fulfilment ... The time for small thinking is
> over because history leaves us no choice.

spluttered Yutar – and was central to the sentences of life imprisonment instead of the death penalty.

Nelson Mandela's address from the dock is rightly remembered as a soaring political statement: a moral and political riposte to the charges brought against himself and his co-accused. But it was only one element in the defence case. Mandela's statement was just that: not led as evidence, and thus not susceptible to cross-examination. It was a different matter for Walter Sisulu and Govan Mbeki, who took the stand and were subjected to days and days of hostile cross-examination by Yutar. Both men acquitted themselves superbly. Sisulu came across (said Joel Joffe, one of his lawyers) as a man 'of tremendous calm, conviction and sincerity'. Mbeki took the stand towards the end of the case. Bram Fischer, for the defence, led him through an account of his life and experience; how he had become involved in politics. Then his evidence ranged from political oppression to social and economic conditions; he covered health, poverty, taxes, wages and the pass laws. The teacher and journalist was on home ground, and delivered a measured and pointed critique of white supremacy.

Cross-examination ensued. Govan's evidence in chief stung Yutar to the quick, his irritation evident from the start. But as the days of cross-examination proceeded, Govan serenely and resolutely held his ground. Did he possess (Yutar quoted from *Spark*) 'a ruthless determination to reach his goal'? 'I spoke the truth,' Govan answered; 'and if you call that ruthless – speaking the truth – then I was ruthless.' He readily admitted that he had held high office in the ANC, in MK and in the Communist Party; that he had been involved in planning acts of sabotage; that he had acted in concert with others; and had envisaged violent revolution. Why then, crowed Yutar, did he not simply plead guilty? 'I did not plead guilty ... for the simple reason, firstly, that I should come and explain from here under oath some of the reasons that led me to join Umkhonto weSizwe. And secondly, for the simple reason that to plead guilty would to my mind indicate a sense of moral guilt to it. I do not accept that there is any moral guilt attached to my actions.'

This rebuttal, like the rest of his evidence, was delivered with an imperturbable calm. He was in the witness box for nearly three days, and Hilda Bernstein provided this memorable vignette: 'Something in Govan's quiet and courteous way of speaking arouses in Yutar a greater antagonism than he has yet displayed to the accused. Pointing a finger at him, Yutar says loudly and angrily: "I want to remind you that this court is trying issues of sabotage and other offences, and it is not a court of inquiry into grievances of the Bantu" ... He attacks Govan for speaking quietly, for being sanctimonious, for appearing to be gentle, and repeats several times that he would "wipe that sanctimonious smile" off Govan's face. He returns again and again to questions of identities, places, names, which Govan refuses to answer ... He is like an angry fly hitting himself again and again against a pane of glass; because the glass is transparent he believes he only has to hit hard enough and he will reach the other side. Govan steadfastly refuses to answer any question which might implicate anyone else.'

Sentences were handed down in the Rivonia trial on Friday 12 June. Rusty Bernstein was found not guilty, but the other eight accused were sentenced to life imprisonment. They were rushed back to Pretoria Local Prison in a police van. Kathrada remembers the heat, the odours of sweat and dust, the fear and aggression on policemen's faces: 'Road signs, stop streets, traffic lights, speed limits – all were ignored in pursuit of locking us away.' Denis Goldberg was taken to the white section of the prison. The others were moved into a communal cell. Emotionally and physically drained by the trial's conclusion, they fell asleep, only to be woken at midnight, and hustled to a military air base. The prisoners were shackled in pairs. Mbeki and Kathrada – oldest and youngest in the group – made their ungainly way up the stairs of a Dakota aircraft, locked to each other by handcuffs and leg-irons. On Saturday 13 June, a cold, wet and windy morning, the plane touched down on the runway on Robben Island.

7

Cold comfort

The Robben Island years

Govan Mbeki spent 23 years and four months in prison – more than a quarter of his long life. His incarceration lasted for 8,522 days: days mapped on the unremitting coordinates of the prison timetable; activities at every waking hour specified by a grid of rules and regulations, strictly applied by one's captors. For almost a quarter of a century, his life was defined by privation, by what was not possible, not permitted, unavailable. The major hardships of prison life are obvious: confinement, loneliness, monotony, the loss of freedom, and the absence of all that was ordinary – taken for granted – in life outside. The petty privations are harder to imagine; but they emerge over and over again in prison memoirs: the daily indignities and discomforts – dress, diet, exhaustion, frustration, the casual harshness and arbitrary vindictiveness of the guards – what Kathrada called a 'litany of degradation'. In an existence that offered so little, punishments were particularly harsh. The food on Robben Island – especially the F Diet given to African prisoners – was unpalatable and at times barely edible. But every warder could impose *drie maaltye* – the loss of all meals for a day – for any perceived infringement. If he had to choose a single word to encapsulate life on the Island, wrote Kathrada, it would be 'cold'. 'Cold food, cold showers, cold winters, cold wind coming in off the cold sea, cold warders, cold cells, cold comfort.'

Every prisoner found different ways of coping. Each experienced his own version of what Saths Cooper called 'the phenomenal human suffering that took place' on Robben Island. Govan Mbeki coped; he survived; but he did so at immense physical and psychic cost. Bram Fischer and Joel Joffe visited the seven Rivonia triallists just after they had been flown to Robben Island, to discuss the prospects of an appeal. Joffe had grown accustomed to Govan's presence during the trial – dignified, controlled, courteous – and it was a particular shock to see him in khaki shorts without underwear and a rough shirt. He 'looked strange and uncomfortable ... He was shivering and cold.' A year later, Mary Benson saw Mbeki when he appeared as a witness in a trial in Humansdorp: 'he had aged considerably and it seemed to me that weariness had settled on him like fine dust.' By the 1980s, Govan's health had deteriorated: high blood pressure, a slipped vertebra and pinched nerve, vision so poor that he could no longer read (happily rectified by operations for glaucoma and cataract) and other ailments took their toll.

The fact that the Robben Island years occupy just one chapter here does not mean that their impact on Mbeki should be underestimated. He wrote to me in August 1988, and in seven typed pages set out 'a sketch of the experiences we went through … on the Island'. All the familiar details are there: prison clothing, food, threadbare blankets in a tiny cell; and the slog of work breaking stones, digging lime, building roads and the new prison – 'that jail was built by us prisoners, with our own hands, we dug the stones, dressed them and laid them … we built a veritable fortress, an ultra-maximum security jail for our own imprisonment.' There are details of violence by named warders; random beatings; the inadequacy of medical treatment; the protracted battles to win minor improvements in conditions; and so on.

He recounted the infamous raid under Lieutenant Fourie in May 1971, when warders stormed the B section (where the Rivonia prisoners and about 20 others were kept, in isolation from the common-law and other political prisoners). 'The order: *staan op, trek uit, teen die muur, hande op*. They were armed with sjamboks and black rubber staves. We stood naked for more than an hour while they searched, threw books and letters and all sorts of papers on the floor. It was cold – bitterly cold. At some stage my arms started jerking high above my head. It was uncontrollable. One warder shouted it was a heart attack – pull him down, he shouted. As I lay on the floor – it was so cold – the bloody sadist of a lieutenant said: do you hear that cannon sound? ... We are giving hell to the Communists – to the Russians. They can't help you, you Communists are cowards.' And he ended the story by adding, 'I won't forget nor forgive that one.' Similarly, after recounting a spell of three months in solitary confinement (for trying to pass a note to the SWAPO prisoner Toivo ya Toivo), he concluded another letter by saying, 'It takes a lot to forgive these things though one may not forget.'

Three aspects of those years merit further mention: Mbeki's absences from the Island when he appeared in other political trials; the political and personal tensions among the Rivonia leadership; and the educational programmes run by the ANC. Govan's testimony infuriated Percy Yutar, as described earlier, but evidently impressed other lawyers. His demeanour under cross-examination, and his mastery of detail, saw him summoned as a defence witness in nine separate political trials. (In fact he was away from the Island for most of two years from 1965 to 1967, so that his prison number was changed to 21/67.) These were cases in Pretoria and Durban (where Sylvia Neame and Harold Strachan faced charges); but also scruffy courts in Cradock, Humansdorp, Addo (twice) and Colesberg, as Eastern Cape activists were rounded up and summarily jailed. In each case, Govan gave expert evidence on the history and policies of the ANC.

These appearances did not endear Mbeki to the prison authorities. At one point 'Brigadier Aucamp told me he was going to keep me away from the Eiland because I was involved in these ANC cases. I thought he was pulling my leg. He meant every word of it. He had me isolated at Colesberg for about ten months, and gave orders to prisoners and warders not to talk to me. And I was only allowed out on exercise, 30 minutes twice daily.' It is unclear whether these absences from Robben Island affected his relations with the others in the single-cell (or B) section, and I was not alert enough to ask him about this. But given that these early years saw routines and personal interactions established, it seems in retrospect likely that Govan's reputation for being a loner on the Island owed something to his belated integration in the section.

Much more significant were the major tensions that developed in the ANC leadership on the Island, when differences over policy and practice were most sharply expressed in deteriorating relations between Mandela and Mbeki. The friction is anatomised in graphic detail in a report to the exiled leadership of the Congress movement. It sought to present 'an accurate summary of the major facts' and announced 'a happy resolution of the whole matter'. None of the scholars who have previously discussed this document have identified its author, but internal evidence suggests that it was almost certainly written by Andrew Masondo.* This also means that the report provided an accurate record, as Masondo told Sifiso Ndlovu that his report to Lusaka 'was certified by the leadership on the Island'. The report described discord in B section, lasting from 1969 to 1975, 'at times reaching extreme tension and bitterness, at times abating in response to efforts to solve it'.

The document explained that the Congress movement's executive structure on the Island was the High Organ. From 1965 to 1972 this comprised Mandela, Mbeki, Mhlaba and Sisulu. The High Organ first split over the question whether the ANC should encourage any involvement in the politics of apartheid structures, such as political parties in the Bantustans, the Coloured Labour Party or the Indian Council. Mandela and Sisulu believed that

* I am grateful to Hugh Macmillan for discussion and correspondence on Masondo as author of the report.

there might be strategic grounds for doing so; the two men from Port Elizabeth were flatly opposed, and cited the resolution to this effect at the Lobatse conference. This division remained constant, 'but the two who represented polar opposites in attitudes and opinions were Madiba and Govan.' A second 'thorny question which though not openly debated was an undercurrent' was the question of Mandela's status: whether the leadership on the Island was collective, or whether Mandela was *primus inter pares*. A third bitter debate bore on the relationship of the ANC and the Communist Party. At one point, the dissenting members of the High Organ were replaced by a different quartet (Z. Bhengu, Masondo, Wilton Mkwayi and Joshua Zulu). The issues were eventually discussed by ANC members beyond the single cells, over the long weekend of Easter 1974; and the matter was sufficiently resolved for the original High Organ to be reinstated.

Why, and how, did this happen? What pitted co-defendants at Rivonia in this stand-off? A partisan explanation lodges responsibility firmly at Govan's door. 'Govan Mbeki, in particular, was the source of bad blood among the principals,' says Padraig O'Malley, biographer of Mac Maharaj. Govan (says Martin Meredith, who never met him) was 'a hard uncompromising communist, intolerant of opposing opinion'. But a more even-handed assessment is necessary; and it would consider views reminding us of Mandela's own capacity for discord. Michael Dingake, in his autobiography, noted that Madiba was said by some to be 'controversial and dogmatic' and that his 'direct, fiercely candid approach' could leave his opponents bloodied and humiliated. Walter Sisulu agreed: 'He could be harsh with colleagues'; Maharaj acknowledged that once Mandela 'had arrived at a position, he was extremely stubborn'; and Masondo recalled how Mandela's interrogatory methods upset the ANC and MK activist Joe Gqabi.

It is worth noting that Masondo's report detailed two earlier attempts at resolving the crisis, in 1970 and 1973. Both were initiated by Mbeki. James April was in B section at the time, and his perception is that although Mhlaba, Gqabi, Masondo and Elias Motsoaledi broadly supported Govan, 'there was no organisation between them'. The opposing group, 'Madiba's group, was organised … it was physically separate, secretive, highly organised', with Kathrada and Maharaj central to its coherence. Others directly involved in the dispute played it down. The whole affair was exaggerated, said Walter Sisulu; there were tensions, but we contained them, said Mhlaba; debates became 'tense and heated', said Kathrada, but never caused a major split. Govan himself agreed: 'from the onset the decision was taken by the High Organ that Nelson would be our spokesman'.

If one moves away from *ex post facto* judgements about the two men, and considers instead the dynamics of the dispute, understanding becomes clearer. Context is crucial. In the enclosed, unnatural confines of prison, minor matters could take root and fester; as Laloo Chiba observed, 'you have arguments, you have quarrels over small things sometimes and relationships sometimes deteriorated.' In 1971, in a smuggled letter, Kathrada confirmed that 'Living with the same faces day in and day out must be having adverse psychological effects … We do get on one another's nerves.' Each clash fed off the previous one; hostility acquired its own momentum. The usual code of confining differences broke down (noted Masondo) and 'individual High Organ men vied with each other and broadcast their mutual recriminations … in a vicious slander campaign'. At the time – to Mandela and Mbeki, to Sisulu and Mhlaba, and to others drawn into the conflict – the stand-off probably seemed to revolve on issues of principle and policy. In retrospect, personality, temperament and the unforgiving context were every bit as important.

A degree of personal rapprochement between Mbeki and Mandela was arrived at in 1977 or 1978. 'Suddenly … Nelson and Govan were walking and talking,' said Sonny Venkatrathnam. 'This was a strange sight to us.' By then both men were responding to a changed political context on the Island, a generational and an ideological challenge. It began with the influx of younger, angry and militant prisoners – the Soweto generation, or *klipgooiers* – and was also affected by the ideological challenge of Black Consciousness, represented on the Island initially by the SASO–BC triallists, and finally by the intake of captured MK guerrillas from the late 1970s. This dramatically altered prison demographic precipitated new levels of political rivalry and hostility on the Island. From 1977 to 1980 the ANC and the PAC sought to recruit followers from among the Black Consciousness Movement (BCM) and the unaffiliated, militant 1976-ers. At times the competition spilled over into scuffles and confrontations. When Terror Lekota left the BCM for the ANC, he was assaulted by outraged colleagues.

By 1980, new protocols on recruitment were agreed between the political movements on the Island, reducing the level of overt hostility. But the various layers of younger prisoners presented another distinct challenge to the Rivonia generation. Govan Mbeki distinguished between the Black Consciousness cohort, 'whose leadership stated they had no time "for the dusty manuscripts of Marx and Engels"', and young ANC and MK members, whose enthusiasm for the national democratic revolution was not matched by knowledge of their own movement's history and policies or the nature of the Congress Alliance. In response the High Organ authorised a systematic programme of political education, compulsory for ANC members on the Island. 'Before the end of 1982', wrote Govan, 'we decided to draw up a syllabus which would be followed throughout the sections.' A historical survey ran from the 19th-century Wars of Dispossession to the present; particular attention was devoted to study of the Freedom Charter, and to 'the reasons for embarking on the armed struggle'. Govan estimated that this syllabus, diligently pursued, would take three years of study. A second syllabus on 'the development of society' provided for a (resoundingly orthodox) outline of Marxist theory and economics.

I have written elsewhere on Govan's prison writings, and his central role in the political education programme of the 1980s,* and will not rehearse that assessment. But a couple of additional issues are worth considering, in the light of two fine studies by Fran Buntman and Philippa Lane and their insights into the question of education on the Island. Prisoners on the Island, particularly ANC prisoners, says Buntman,

---

* Colin Bundy, 'Introduction', *Learning from Robben Island: The Prison Writings of Govan Mbeki.*

'self-consciously developed and cultivated the belief that their prison was a "university", a training ground for young leaders, a lecture podium for the most senior leaders ... a tolerant community in which pluralism respected all political movements, and a center of such profound and essential correctness that even warders and criminals could be converted to the "cause"'.

She and Lane both quote Saths Cooper, who resisted the romanticisation of prison life and was sceptical in particular of the tag 'university'. They are right to avoid uncritical embrace of the claims that are today so prominent in the tourist and heritage industries and the Robben Island Museum's presentations. But Buntman's treatment of the political education programme as a key instance of 'strategic resistance' on the Island is persuasive. What the programme *sought* to achieve was 'that prisoners expend time and energy developing themselves and their organisations ... Enhancing the liberation movements demanded knowledgeable and disciplined members of organizations who could, upon release, rejuvenate, support, or redirect external antiapartheid struggles. This was what a good graduate of Robben Island was meant to do ...'

Quite apart from the political education programme, political prisoners on the Island were committed to learning in general. 'If you do not watch out,' warned Natoo Babenia, 'prison can put your brain to death' – and he told how important cultural activities (plays, music, board games, organised sport) were, and how being able to teach 'brought new enthusiasm into one's life', from literacy classes – 'we got to 100%' – to arithmetic, bookkeeping and other subjects at matric level. Michael Dingake and others told how, although it involved physical hardship, work in the lime quarry also provided time and space for intense discussions, an unlikely 'site for intellectual stimulation'.

The two names mentioned most often by ex-prisoners when they referred to teaching on the island were Neville Alexander and Govan Mbeki. Both men were graduates; and both made use of the limited opportunities available to study. Govan wrote Standard 6 Afrikaans shortly after arriving on the Island, and in the following year wrote and passed Afrikaans at Junior Certificate level. He studied 3rd-year Economics through Unisa, and then Honours in Economics. After that he could only take single subjects – he did three years of Business Economics – and fought a protracted and finally unsuccessful struggle to register for a Master's degree. In addition to these endeavours on his own behalf, Govan was involved in teaching others at levels from basic literacy to Bachelor's degrees. 'We encouraged people to study,' he recalled. 'It is good for them. It is good for our discipline too.'

Govan's involvement in the formal education and political education programmes meant a great deal to him during his last decade on the Island. Music was another source of pleasure. In 1973 Mbeki acquired a guitar – and as he wrote to his grandson Karl Mbeki in 1980 – 'I don't play it well but I get a great deal of satisfaction from the little I can manage to play.' There is an evocative passage in his interview with Bridget Thompson when Govan discusses musical forms and melodies, ranging from Xhosa folksongs and lullabies, through compositions by Tiyo Soga and Tyamzashe, to tangos and waltzes, jazz by Count Basie and the Dark Town Strutters – and more. Music involved others. 'Now I used to play the lead guitar, there were three of us … the bass, now it was Don Davis, you know he picked the bass strings of the guitar at the upper end. And then Neville, Neville Alexander, then he used to start … We played all sorts of things. Like *boeremusiek*, "Sarie Marais", and "Suikerbossie", and "Hasie, hoekom is jou stert so kort?".'

Such interaction was significant, as Govan tended not to become involved in other forms of recreation. He was too old for most organised sporting activities, although he refereed some volleyball games. He identified himself as an atheist, and eschewed the church services (even though some attended these for the contact with others that they provided.) Thami Mkhwanazi recalled that Govan 'never went to film shows' and watched television only for the news. These choices shaped memories of Oom Gov on the Island – memories, wrote Gevisser, 'of his remoteness, his distance, his desire for solitude, and his particular combination of civility, certitude, and what South Africans call *koppigheid*'. Govan never warmed to the PAC prisoners in his section, and did not encourage political discussions and debates with non-ANC structures. Kader Hassim believed he was right 'because I think he realised nobody is going to change and when you go to prison you become even more rigid there than you are outside'. If Govan recognised this in others, they surely did in him. His views and behaviour became more rigid and less accommodating. The rift within the High Organ may have been formally resolved, but was never fully healed. The emotional distance between Mbeki and the other Rivonia prisoners became a physical divide: in March 1982 Mandela, Sisulu, Mhlaba and Mlangeni were moved to Pollsmoor on the mainland, and Kathrada followed them in October of the same year. Mbeki's tendencies to solitude increased, and, one may surmise, so did his loneliness.

Beginning in 1980 (when the restrictions governing correspondence had somewhat relaxed) Govan Mbeki wrote a series of letters to his daughter-in-law Dot Lewis, Moeletsi's ex-wife, and his grandson Karl Govan Mbeki ('my young namesake and my old teacher's namesake'). During his last five years on the Island, Dot and Karl became Govan's most frequent visitors, seeing him every year in December or January. His letters to them are very moving, his growing affection unfeigned and explicit. He was delighted by the fact that they met other members of his family, travelling to Idutywa to meet Piny; and he revelled in the warmth of Piny's praise of their grandson: 'a fine young man, soft-spoken and considerate'. Censorship of prisoners' letters had relaxed by the 1980s, and only one of his letters to Karl is defaced by a warder blacking out a passage. Govan finds ways of discussing the governments of Thatcher and Reagan, which he detested; but also the British miners' strike ('King Arthur must be keeping everybody jumping'!) and the women at Greenham Common, whom he applauded. He devotes a great deal of the correspondence to Karl's education, devouring the teenager's school reports with enthusiasm.

Almost entirely absent from letters over many years is any reference to circumstances in prison. This may have reflected regulations restricting such comments, but the topic seems to have been off bounds for Govan himself. He breached this just twice. Karl was a keen sea-scout, and sent his grandfather a birthday card with a picture of a sailboat. Govan thanked him and added, 'But I promise you I'm not going to sail away from where I am!' In 1981 Govan wrote to Dot, apologising for being impatient in wanting to hear from her: he realised that people 'in the other world than mine' had much to keep them busy, and 'One does tend to understand. But that is only momentary sweet reasonableness. Here on my side of the barred divide there isn't much variety to spread one's attention. Today hardly differs from yesterday and there is little prospect that tomorrow will be any different. There are times when I miss fish and chips like hell …' It is hard to say which is more poignant: the bleak sense of monotony or the unexpected codicil, with its whiff of vinegar.

8

Release, retirement – and a modest revolutionary?

Govan Mbeki's release from prison was not straightforward in its planning, execution or consequences. All the Rivonia triallists had previously rejected conditional offers of release, Govan as recently as 1985. By 1987, however, Nelson Mandela was meeting government ministers and securocrats – early engagements in talks about talks, negotiating towards negotiations. Mandela won a split-vote approval for these talks from his colleagues at Pollsmoor (Mhlaba and Mlangeni in favour, Sisulu with reservations, and Kathrada opposed), and had advised Tambo in Lusaka of his dealings, but was flying solo. This carried its own risks, as became evident.

Mandela urged the Minister of Justice, Kobie Coetsee, to release unconditionally the oldest Rivonia triallists, Mbeki and Sisulu. The government was concerned about Mbeki's health – a free Rivonia 'lifer' was preferable to a Rivonia 'lifer' dying on Robben Island – and eventually acceded. Govan knew nothing of these dealings when he was abruptly moved from B section into solitary quarters in August 1987. His lawyer, Priscilla Jana, was refused permission to see him, and promptly sought a court order to gain access to her client. This was just a week before the planned release. The authorities were livid, and threatened to cancel the release. Mandela scrambled a compromise, which involved having Mbeki brought to the mainland for a face-to-face briefing, so that Jana would drop the court action. It was not an easy meeting for either man. Mandela 'was less than open with Mbeki' (wrote Allister Sparks later): yes, he was negotiating, but, no, he could not give any details; he also told Govan that 'Walter and the others didn't know either'. Govan cautiously agreed to proceed with the release as planned; met again with Mandela on the day of his release; and later told Sparks that he was unhappy Mandela did not 'have sufficient confidence in me to tell me the full story'.

Early on the morning of 5 November 1987, warders brought Govan a grey suit, shirt, tie, socks and shoes. He was taken to Pollsmoor for a medical check-up and the meeting with Mandela, who, reported Anthony Sampson, 'advised Mbeki to act with restraint'. He was then flown to Port Elizabeth, and ushered without much notice into a press conference to face some 200 journalists from print and broadcast media. He had prepared no statement or speech, so simply answered questions. Yes, he was still an active member of the ANC; and, yes, of the Communist Party too. He would continue 'to support MK as long as the ANC deems it necessary' – and he urged youth in the townships 'to continue with the struggle'. After a second press conference in Johannesburg, he returned to Port Elizabeth, and entered New Brighton.

A report in the *Weekly Mail* captures the mood of the day: 'all traffic laws were liberated. People hung out of the sides of fast-moving taxis, children and old women danced on the sidewalks and crowds of people toyi-toyied'. *Baba uMbeki Yinkoledi* (Father Mbeki is our leader), they sang. The authorities rapidly decided that they had seen enough of the intransigent Mbeki and the fervour he elicited. A rally in the Dan Qeqe Stadium was banned; the Minister of Law and Order, Adriaan Vlok, grumbled that he had hoped Mbeki would 'quietly retire' – and sought to hasten this by serving a banning order on him. This imposed a 12-hour house arrest, confined him to Port Elizabeth magistracy, and prohibited Mbeki's being quoted or involved in anything intended for publication.

There was a final episode of the long-running

story of tensions between Mbeki (still bristling with suspicion) and Mandela (increasingly revered and beyond critique). In March 1989, a partial text of Mandela's letter to P.W. Botha sped round underground circuits. Govan, like others in the UDF/ Mass Democratic Movement, was alarmed that too much was on offer without prior consultation; and he urged activists to cut contacts with Madiba. Mac Maharaj intervened, successfully, to reassure Govan and others that Mandela was acting with the ANC's full approval. Maharaj was also critical of Govan's efforts to create an underground network (including as members Kgalema Motlanthe and Cyril Ramaphosa), which he believed compromised Operation Vula.

By 1990, the state remained militarily powerful, but had lost legitimacy. The liberation movement was politically powerful, but militarily ineffectual. Both came to a reluctant recognition of this stalemate. The dynamics set in train by Mandela's release in February 1990 prioritised negotiations over underground organisation or mass mobilisation. Grassroots activism was effectively put on hold, irrelevant to the new phase.

In June 1991 the ANC's National Conference was held in Durban. Govan's withdrawal from active politics was manifest in his decision not to stand for election to the National Executive Committee. He turned his energies, instead, to writing. In April and May of that year, he worked on a Xhosa-language manual for use by ANC Political Study Groups (which Pallo Jordan recalls as very useful); and he was also completing the text of what was published as *The Struggle for Liberation in South Africa: A Short History*. Govan began work on this history of resistance in 1988. In a letter in June 1989, he complained that he was 'moving much too slow' on the manuscript: 'things being equal I expect to be through with it in the next six to nine months. By the time I am 80 I want to be free to relax a bit.'

And, by degrees, Govan's life became more relaxed, less driven, as the 1990s proceeded. *The Struggle for Liberation* was published in May 1992. Later that year, he obtained funding from the University of Amsterdam, which made it possible to employ five postgraduate researchers at Fort Hare. They worked on a study of the years from 1963 to 1993, which was published in 1996 as *Sunset at Midday*.* He travelled beyond southern Africa for the first time in his life: in 1991 he spent a couple of months in Europe; in 1992 he travelled to Canada and to Dakar, where he was

* Although Govan Mbeki appears as author, *Sunset at Midday* was largely researched by postgraduate students at Fort Hare and in Port Elizabeth; Rok Ajulu prepared the work for publication; Lindiwe Sisulu was seconded by the ANC to oversee the project.

awarded the Amilcar Cabral Prize. In 1994 Govan was appointed Deputy President of the Senate, an essentially ceremonial office. It did involve considerable further travel, including three trips to the Far East. He was allocated official housing in the parliamentary complex on the Groote Schuur estate, and split his time between Cape Town and Port Elizabeth. He read (mostly non-fiction); the only writing in these twilight years was letters, and he remained a diligent correspondent; he welcomed visitors with every sign of enjoyment; he gave considered, thoughtful interviews to scholars and journalists; and he indulged his love of music. He was delighted to accept an invitation to become the Patron-in-Chief of the Cape Town Symphony Orchestra. Zubeida Jaffer has left an enchanting picture of attending a concert in Cape Town with Govan and Mamisa Chabula (his doctor and by then also his closest confidante): 'Oom Gov in his dark suit, white cuff-linked shirt and pinned tie, his head held high, strides into the City Hall and up its winding stairs with us on either side. His pleasure is palpable: not bad at all for an old man to be flanked by two younger women. His eyes have softened and he chuckles to himself.' And that is where this biography chooses to leave Oom Gov: free to relax a bit.

*

Govan Mbeki in Port Elizabeth, 1990. (© Eastern Province Herald)

But what is Govan Mbeki's place in history? What did he achieve? How should he be remembered? These are the questions asked of any life story and its subject. Obvious questions, perhaps, but not ones that yield easy answers. As a young graduate, already an ANC member, Mbeki drafted *Transkei in the Making* in 1937. From that time, he had close links with Communist Party activists – and, of course, married one. Also early in his career, Mbeki's distinctive point of departure took shape: that peasants and migrant workers in the Reserves should be taken seriously by nationalist and Marxist movements. Fully 60 years later, he was still at work: dividing his time between duties as Deputy President of the Senate and clocking in to the ANC offices when he was in Port Elizabeth.

Despite this political longevity, there is a sceptical, even hostile, view of Govan Mbeki surfacing in scholarly treatments of South Africa's political history. It is encapsulated in David Smith's *Young Mandela*. Without any attribution, the author remarks: 'People would be suspicious, later, that Govan had seemed to ascend so rapidly within the ANC, without ever paying his due in terms of bannings and arrests.' And the case is made more fully – partly by innuendo, partly by wilful selectivity – in Padraig O'Malley's biography of Mac Maharaj. 'It is a matter of inquiry as to when Govan Mbeki became a member of the

ANC. In his diaries ... Mandela has a note referring to Mbeki's membership: "G. became active in the ANC when he left teaching in 1955 ... He became speaker [i.e., chairman at the annual conference] in 1958 when the hard core of the ANC leadership were unavailable by bans and the Treason Trial ... Of some puzzlement, too, is the fact that Mbeki ... was only banned in 1962; was not himself among the Treason Trialists ... Thus from the 1940s or earlier the first time he came to the attention of the security agencies was in late 1962 ...'"

This 'puzzlement' arises only by a failure to acknowledge items of Mbeki's history that are in the public realm: that he joined the ANC in 1935; that when he made friends with Walter Sisulu in 1938, the two young men moved in ANC circles in Johannesburg; that he was a member of the committee that drafted the rights document *Africans' Claims* for the ANC in 1943; that he was in frequent correspondence with Dr Xuma, President-General of the ANC during the 1940s; that (as Mandela wrote in his autobiography) Govan 'had been deeply involved in the planning of the Congress of the People'; or that (like Raymond Mhlaba) he was named as a co-conspirator at the Treason Trial. Far from only appearing on the security radar for the first time in 'late 1962', Govan had been sacked three times as a teacher and blacklisted for other posts on political grounds since the late 1930s.

(Not in the public domain, but evident in the archives, is that Govan was under surveillance, his mail opened and his movements followed, as early as the mid-1940s.)

If the suspicions and puzzlement may be set aside, the questions remain: exactly how does one sum up so long a career; what patterns are discernible? Can the subject of any biography be categorised, pinned down, to any satisfactory extent – or does any attempt to do so impose artificial limits and arbitrary meanings? While fully recognising how much of Mbeki's life such an exercise omits or occludes, I would propose that his achievements and legacy may be distilled so as to consider him as a writer, as a teacher, and as a revolutionary.

Writer
Excessive claims are made on Mbeki's behalf. A leading on-line history site says that *The Peasants' Revolt* 'was a major historical study of peasant struggles' – which it was not – and concludes with a flourish, 'Indeed, he was one of the great Marxist writers of the previous century' – which he was not. He was variously a pamphleteer, polemicist and reporter; when he had time to devote himself to the task, he was a commentator, essayist, analyst and author. I suspect that he viewed his exertions across these categories

as fairly seamless: in almost everything he wrote, the written word was deployed as part of a broader social and political project. As a journalist, Govan was more than a reporter, although some of the stories he filed for *New Age* were exemplary reportage, combining vivid detail and incisive analysis. His most telling journalism – in *Inkundla*, the *Guardian*, *Fighting Talk* and *Liberation* – was a sustained attempt to understand and reveal the political economy of the Transkei.

That project began in Mbeki's early booklet *Transkei in the Making*, and found greater focus and depth in several articles for the *Territorial Magazine/Inkundla* and especially in the three-part study 'Government Plan for Native Reserves' in the *Guardian* in April and May 1945. These articles focused on the nexus of migrant labour, rural poverty, landlessness and overstocking. They characterised a rural proletariat as a reserve army of labour and contrasted the bland language of 'rehabilitation' with the grim social realities of the landless poor. This line of analysis was updated and sharpened in the *Liberation* series discussed in Chapter 5, and elaborated most fully in *The Peasants' Revolt*. The cumulative importance of these writings is substantial. They are the most innovative, and most durable, of all Mbeki's output. To appreciate Mbeki's prescience, one need only think of how central to the revisionist historiography of the 1970s was the role of migrancy and of the Reserves in creating and sustaining a reserve army of labour, or the potency of the 'dumping ground' metaphor in studies of forced removals.

I asked Govan once about his theoretical contribution to Marxist thought in South Africa, and he waved the question aside self-deprecatingly: 'No, no, Michael Harmel, he was a theorist. Not me.' This is broadly true. Govan was not primarily a theorist. Yet there is a striking formulation in the *Liberation* series, styling the relationship of the Reserves to modern South Africa as one of 'introverted colonialism'. Although arrived at quite independently, it is analytically analogous to the Party's subsequent, and better known, 'Colonialism of a Special Type'. Ruth First (supporting the award of an honorary degree to Govan by the University of Amsterdam) noted that he had seen the Bantustans as a neo-colonial solution, requiring a collaborating class. 'The prophetic force of [*Peasants' Revolt*] is really incredible ... he provides a detailed analysis of how the class structure in the Transkei could contribute to such collaboration.' She may have overstated the case but accurately identified the most original arguments in the book.

Teacher

Govan often referred to his training, practice and identity as a teacher. In a note written to a younger prisoner on Robben Island, he cheerfully admitted his schoolmasterly way: 'You complain that my Note was full of "provocative assertions, hints and undeveloped points" which have set your mind athinking. Blame my training as a teacher ... One of the most important lessons ... was the injunction to draw the answers from the pupils. They should work out answers from the hints thrown out. When I write I so often forget that my position is no longer that of a teacher.'

His relish for the classroom was unmistakable. Bridget Thompson, in the making of her film *Heart and Stone*, asked Govan what it meant to be involved in the educational programmes on Robben Island. 'You know, it was such a pleasure ... We prepared a document, it gets circulated ... At some stage you get a feedback, somebody is posing questions ... someone is not satisfied and he would write back wanting a further explanation ... It was thrilling. It's like a teacher in the classroom ... you go into the classroom, you start a lesson, and they all sit there with blank faces. You start delivering the lesson and one by one it's like stars in the sky: you see one star come up – one by one these faces brighten up all of a sudden ... And you realize that what you are trying to put across is being appreciated, it is being understood.'

In several different interviews, Govan fondly recalled his days as a school teacher. He told Sifiso Ndlovu that he had to balance his formal responsibilities as a teacher with his extracurricular political activities: 'And so I adopted an attitude where I gave everything as a teacher inside the classroom – as a Latin master, Physical Science teacher, Psychology of Education and Principles of Education [at Clarkebury] plus teaching Xhosa, Physiology and Hygiene … I gave everything that I had in the classroom so that I should not be blamed for not paying attention to my work as a teacher on the grounds that I was spending too much time preaching politics outside the classroom … I never had a single failure in all the subjects I have mentioned, both at High School and at the Training School … in the few years as a teacher I never had a failure in my class. Thank you, I wanted to add that.'

Rather like his writings, Govan's efforts as teacher were also bound closely up with his politics, and particularly with the project of systematic political education, commenced in Port Elizabeth and then transplanted onto the Island. Govan explained the connection in matter-of-fact terms. He arrived in Port Elizabeth in 1955, he said, where 'they had built a core during the Defiance Campaign of what was known as the Volunteers ... This was a group of ordinary men and women – virtually all of them from the working class ... I came in as a teacher and my view was to draw from experience as a teacher, how do you educate? ... I felt we needed to bring into the ANC those methods.'

Kathy Kathrada made the same connection. 'Govan was a teacher, not only in his choice of profession, but in essence and soul.' When he moved to Port Elizabeth, already an ANC stronghold, what was lacking 'was a systematic programme of political education, and Govan filled that vacuum'.

Revolutionary

Many of the critical adjectives applied to Govan Mbeki – hard, uncompromising, rigid, ruthless – are also conventionally attributed to 'revolutionaries'. And there is *some* correspondence between aspects of Mbeki's personality and behaviour, on the one hand, and his political beliefs and actions, on the other. Earlier chapters have traced this convergence and suggested how political context and exigencies shaped Mbeki, rendering him more resolute and less forgiving, commitment trumping compassion. But explaining personality in terms of politics, or vice versa, is a limited exercise. It is more fruitful to establish what comprises revolutionary politics and to consider Mbeki's career in this light.

It is clear that Mbeki was a committed member of the Communist Party; he believed that ending national oppression was a necessary first step, but that real liberation required the end of capitalist exploitation. In the polemics on Robben Island, Govan was a leader of the 'Communists' in their debates with the 'nationalists'. As his surviving prison writings indicate, what was at stake was the transfer of power 'from the bourgeoisie and its henchmen, into the hands of … the dominated classes'. To this end 'a strong working class party … strong in members and single-minded in purpose' was a prerequisite. He warned that a negotiated outcome might see capital 'draw into its service sections of the oppressed who will go out … to preach the dawn of a new era of fulfilment' and insisted that to strengthen capitalism at the end of the liberation struggle would be 'a retrograde step, rather than a progressive one'.

Ciraj Rassool's thoughtful critique of South African political biography warns against an approach that constructs 'national histories in which leaders have been made to speak as national subjects'. I agree with him that resistance history (and biography) is often teleological, and with Jonathan Hyslop that there is a strong tendency to serve up 'an official narrative of the liberation struggle, centred on the ANC and its leadership'. So I want to resist the temptation to vest

Mbeki's radicalism with retrospective coherence and continuity, or to see it as moving ineluctably to the desired outcome; and instead to identify some of its contradictions.

Firstly, although Mbeki emphasised the separate political role of the Communist Party, he was also at pains to valorise the alliance between the ANC and the CP. This meant accepting that the CP, in theory and in practice, prioritised the national question over class struggle, defining its own priorities as promoting the interests of the ANC. Far from insisting on the vanguard role normally claimed by Communist parties, the SACP was happy to allocate this to the ANC. This position was maintained throughout the years the Party operated in exile. Then, back on home ground in the early 1990s (against the backdrop of the collapse of the Soviet system), the Party maintained a rhetorical commitment to the national democratic revolution and a practical acquiescence in the ANC's choice of the capitalist road. With the election of the ANC in 1994, 'two-stage theory' relegated working-class interests to an indefinite future, a second socialist stage postponed *sine die*. There was an inescapable dilemma for orthodox Communists in this outcome; and Mbeki was impaled on it.

Secondly, Mbeki's reputation as a revolutionary was, for many young cadres, immeasurably enhanced by his role in the turn to armed struggle and as the co-author of 'Operation Mayibuye'. Yet in terms of desired revolutionary outcomes, armed struggle *in the form it assumed* was conspicuously unsuccessful. When the Congress Alliance launched armed struggle, it prioritised military action as *the* key element in the struggle for national liberation. It assumed that armed activity by a small MK force would detonate broader political revolt against the state. For 20 years, the ANC relied on military exploits to develop political bases inside the country. Correspondingly, it neglected underground activism and semi-legal forms of struggle inside the country. This locked the exile movement into a fundamental dilemma: without an internal base, it was difficult to mount armed struggle; but without the demonstration effect of military combat, it was equally hard to build a domestic revolutionary base.

Thirdly, Govan and others in the Port Elizabeth ANC and Party structures were understandably proud of the strength and depth of their militant membership; but with historical hindsight the movements paid a terrible price for their success. In the aftermath of Rivonia, the state sought to stamp out organised resistance, and did so by the arrest of second- and third-echelon activists and a relentless series of court cases. But nowhere were these as numerous as in the Eastern Cape where (wrote Mary Benson) the security police were 'intent on purging Port Elizabeth's townships, New Brighton and Kwazakele … of the last drop of political consciousness'. From 1963 to 1966, some 1,700 men and women were tried in the Eastern Cape in 220 separate cases, charged with furthering the aims of the ANC or, in a few cases, the PAC. These cases followed a grim pattern: held *in camera* in remote locations; evidence given by 'professional' witnesses, traipsed from court to court; details fabricated to a ludicrous extent; many of those charged unrepresented, their cases not reported. Their cumulative effect was to shatter the ANC and Party presence so diligently constructed.

Finally, Govan's very constancy – his adamant advocacy of a distinct role for the Party throughout the Robben Island exchanges – arguably disabled him politically once negotiations began. Commenting on a draft of the 'Inqindi–Marxism' document, drawn up in about 1980 in an attempt to settle the argument, Mbeki scoffed at the idea that 'the liberatory forces could find some accommodation with the bourgeoisie to implement the Freedom Charter'. If the ANC were 'to set up a bourgeois democracy after freedom it would be to entrench capitalism to the detriment of the oppressed.' By the early 1990s, these views were out of step with what was happening in the committee rooms of CODESA. They were also at odds with a negotiated outcome that achieved sweeping political change alongside broad continuity in economic terms. Whatever cogency they retain in retrospect, Govan's distrust of a bourgeois democracy had little purchase at the time.

The closest he came to spelling out his reservations about the process was in the closing passages of *Sunset at Midday*. The negotiated outcome was 'a war without absolute winners'; Afrikaner nationalism and African nationalism 'had fought to a draw'. The ANC was prepared 'to enter into a spirit of compromise'; it 'bent over backwards' to accommodate other political players. The Government of National Unity was 'a reflection of these compromises'. Revolutions, 'even modest ones, are made not in our dreams but in concrete, historical situations. What we have achieved, although far from perfect, is a starting point.' The language is far from triumphalist. It is shot through with a sense of making the best of it: of compromise, of achievement short of victory – the old revolutionary comforting himself that it had been, after all, a modest revolution.

158

To My Grandfather
by Karl Mbeki

If someone were to ask me
what it's like to visit Robben Island
I would tell them to ask another question
If someone were to ask me what it's
like to visit a relation who has
already done twenty-one years
in prison and is looking at doing the same again
I would tell the person the visiting
room is a wide corridor split down
the middle with a thick, sound-proof
wall, there are fourteen cubicles and
you look through a tiny double
glazed window with a movable
steel plate in the middle
I would tell the person that the
way you talk is through a telephone
with a warder listening in
I would tell that person that they will
run out of things to say after three
minutes and it's embarrassing when
you've waited a year to see the person
If someone were to ask me what it
feels like to sit on a hard bench and talk for three hours
down a phone
I would tell that person that when
they leave they will want a wheelchair
as the whole experience is extremely
physically and mentally tiring
I would tell that person that after
having a telephone receiver pressed

hard against an ear for two hours
your arm turns to jelly and your
ear feels like it's got a hundred
pounds hanging from the lobe
And then, after telling that person
what it's like
I would tell that person that the only
thing you can feel coming off a
seventy-two-year-old who's nearly
spent a quarter of a century behind
bars is strength
Strength radiates from behind his thick glasses
Strength radiates from his arthritic hands
Strength radiates from his grey hair
Strength radiates from his jaw line
Strength radiates from his soul
Strength radiates

© Jenny Altshuler

Bibliography

This reading list includes all the printed sources cited or quoted in the text, plus a few that were drawn upon but not cited. Apart from my own interviews with Govan Mbeki, I also used those by Bridget Thompson in the making of her film *Heart and Stone*, and by Gillian Hart, Sifiso Ndlovu, Padraig O'Malley, Rory Riordan and Charles Villa-Vicencio.

On or by Govan Mbeki

Bartlema, Rob and Johan Kortenray, *Govan Mbeki*, in United Nations Center Against Apartheid, *Notes and Documents*, August 1978 (transl. from article in the University of Amsterdam's *Folia Civitas*, 24 December 1977)

Bundy, Colin, 'Introduction', in *Learning from Robben Island: The Prison Writings of Govan Mbeki* by Govan Mbeki (David Philip, Cape Town, 1991)

Gevisser, Mark, *Thabo Mbeki: The Dream Deferred* (Jonathan Ball, Johannesburg, 2007)

Mbeki, Govan, *Transkei in the Making* (Verulam Press, 1939)

Mbeki, Govan, *Let's Do It Together!* (The African Bookman, Cape Town, 1944)

Mbeki, Govan, *South Africa, The Peasants' Revolt* (International Defence and Aid Fund for Southern Africa, London, 1984; first published 1964 by Penguin)

Mbeki, Govan, *Learning from Robben Island: The Prison Writings of Govan Mbeki* (David Philip, Cape Town, 1991)

Mbeki, Govan, *The Struggle for Liberation in South Africa: A Short History* (David Philip, Cape Town, 1992)

Mbeki, Govan, *Sunset at Midday: Latshon'ilang'emini!* (Nolwazi Educational Publishers, Braamfontein, 1996)

On the Rivonia raid and Rivonia trial

Bernstein, Hilda, *The World That Was Ours: The Story of the Rivonia Trial* (Persephone Books, London, 2004; first published 1967 by Heinemann)

Bernstein, Rusty, *Memory Against Forgetting* (Viking, London, 1999)

Bizos, George, *Odyssey to Freedom* (Random House, Cape Town, 2007)

Broun, Kenneth, *Saving Nelson Mandela: The Rivonia Trial and the Fate of South Africa* (Oxford University Press, Oxford, 2012)

Joffe, Joel, *The State vs Nelson Mandela: The Trial That Changed South Africa* (Oneworld, Oxford, 2007)

Kantor, James, *A Healthy Grave* (Hamish Hamilton, London, 1967)

Magubane, Ben, Phil Bonner, Jabulani Sithole, Peter Delius, Janet Cherry, Pat Gibbs and Thozama April, 'The Turn to Armed Struggle', in *The Road to Democracy in South Africa*, SADET, vol. 1: *1960–1970*, pp. 53–146 (Zebra Press, Cape Town, 2004)

On Robben Island

Alexander, Neville, *Robben Island Dossier 1964–1974* (University of Cape Town Press, Rondebosch, 1994)

Banenia, Natoo, *Memoirs of a Saboteur* (Mayibuye Books, Bellville, 1995)

Buntman, Fran, *Robben Island and Prisoner Resistance to Apartheid* (Cambridge University Press, Cambridge, 2003)

Daniels, Eddie, *There and Back: Robben Island 1964–1979* (Mayibuye Books, Bellville, 1998)

Deacon, Harriet (ed.), *The Island: A History of Robben Island 1488–1990* (David Philip and Mayibuye, Cape Town and Bellville, 1996)

Dingake, Michael, *My Fight Against Apartheid* (Kliptown Books, London, 1987)

Kathrada, Ahmed, *Memoirs* (Zebra Press, Cape Town 2004)

Lane, Phillipa, '"Heroes as Ordinary People": A Social and Cultural History of Political Imprisonment in South Africa, 1960–1992' (PhD thesis, University of Essex, 2009)

Maharaj, Mac (ed.), *Reflections in Prison* (Zebra Press and Robben Island Museum, Cape Town, 2001)

Penn, Nigel, Harriet Deacon and Neville Alexander (eds.), *Robben Island: The Politics of Rock and Sand* (UCT, Department of Adult Education and Extra-mural Studies, Cape Town, 1992)

Solani, Noel and Noor Nieftagodien, 'Political Imprisonment and Resistance in South Africa: The Case of Robben Island, 1960–1970', in *The Road to Democracy in South Africa*, SADET, vol. 1, pp. 391–410 (Zebra Press, Cape Town, 2004)

Other memoirs, autobiographies and biographies

Benson, Mary, *A Far Cry: The Making of a South African* (Penguin, London, 1989)

Coko: Reminiscences of Joseph Scotch Coko, edited by Richard Moyer (Institute of Social and Economic Research, Rhodes University, Grahamstown, 1973)

Lodge, Tom, *Mandela: A Critical Life* (Oxford University Press, Oxford, 2006)

Mandela, Nelson, *Long Walk to Freedom: The Autobiography of Nelson Mandela* (Macdonald Purnell, Randburg, 1994)

Meredith, Martin, *Nelson Mandela: A Biography* (Hamish Hamilton, London, 1997)

Ntantala, Phyllis, *A Life's Mosaic: The Autobiography of Phyllis Ntantala* (University of California Press, Berkeley, 1993)

O'Malley, Padraig, *Shades of Difference: Mac Maharaj and the Struggle for South Africa* (Viking, New York 2007)

Raymond Mhlaba's Personal Memoirs: Reminiscences from Rwanda and Uganda, narrated to Thembeka Mufamadi (HSRC Press and Robben Island Museum, Pretoria and Cape Town, 2001)

Sampson, Anthony, *Mandela: The Authorised Biography* (Harper Collins, London, 1999)

Sisulu, Elinor, *Walter and Albertina Sisulu: In Our Lifetime* (David Philip, Cape Town, 2002)

Smith, David James, *Young Mandela* (Phoenix, London, 2010)

Strachan, Harold, *Make a Skyf, Man!* (Jacana, Johannesburg, 2004)

Turok, Ben, *Nothing but the Truth: Behind the ANC's Struggle Politics* (Jonathan Ball, Johannesburg, 2003)

South African history and politics

Baines, Gary, 'Community Resistance and Collective Violence: The Port Elizabeth Defiance Campaign and the 1952 New Brighton Riots', *South African Historical Journal* 34 (1996) 39–76

Cherry, Janet, 'Traditions and Transitions: African Political Participation in Port Elizabeth' (Paper presented at Wits History Workshop, 1994)

Cherry, Janet, 'The Myth of Working Class Defeat: Port Elizabeth in the Post-war Years', *Kronos* 30 (1993)

Gerhart, Gail and Clive Glaser (eds.), *From Protest to Challenge: A Documentary History of African Politics in South Africa, 1882–1990*, vol. 6: *Challenge and Victory, 1980–1990* (Indiana University Press, Bloomington, 2010)

Hart, Gillian, *Disabling Globalization: Places of Power in Post-Apartheid South Africa* (University of Natal Press, Pietermaritzburg, 2002)

Hyslop, Jonathan, 'On Biography: A Response to Ciraj Rassool', *South African Review of Sociolog*, 41, 2 (2010)

Karis, Thomas, Gwendolyn Carter and Gail Gerhart (eds.), *From Protest to Challenge: A Documentary History of African Politics in South Africa, 1882–1990*, vol. 3: *Challenge and Violence, 1953–1964* (Stanford, Hoover Institution Press, 1977)

Karis, Thomas and Gail Gerhart (eds.), *From Protest to Challenge: A Documentary History of African Politics in South Africa, 1882–1990*, vol. 5: *Nadir and Resurgence, 1964–1979* (Indiana University Press, Bloomington, 1997)

Kepe, Thembela and Lungisile Ntsebeza (eds.), *Rural Resistance in South Africa: The Mpondo Revolts after Fifty Years* (Brill, Leiden, 2011)

Lodge, Tom, *Black Politics in South Africa since 1954* (Longman, London, 1983)

Lodge, Tom, *Sharpeville: An Apartheid Massacre and Its Consequences* (Oxford University Press, Oxford, 2011)

Matoti, Sukudu and Lungisile Ntsebeza, 'Rural Resistance in Mpondoland and Thembuland, 1960–63', in *The Road to Democracy in South Africa*, SADET, vol. 1, pp.177–108 (Zebra Press, Cape Town, 2004)

Rassool, Ciraj, 'Rethinking Documentary History and South African Political Biography', *South African Review of Sociology*, 41, 1 (2010), 28–55

SADET, *The Road to Democracy in South Africa*, vol. 1: *1960–1970* (Zebra Press, Cape Town, 2004)

SADET, *The Road to Democracy: South Africans Telling Their Stories*, vol. 1: *1950–1970* (Tsehai Publishers, Hollywood, 2008)

Shubin, Vladimir, *ANC: A View from Moscow* (Mayibuye Books, Bellville, 1999)

Index